Travellers' guide to Kenya and Northern Tanzania

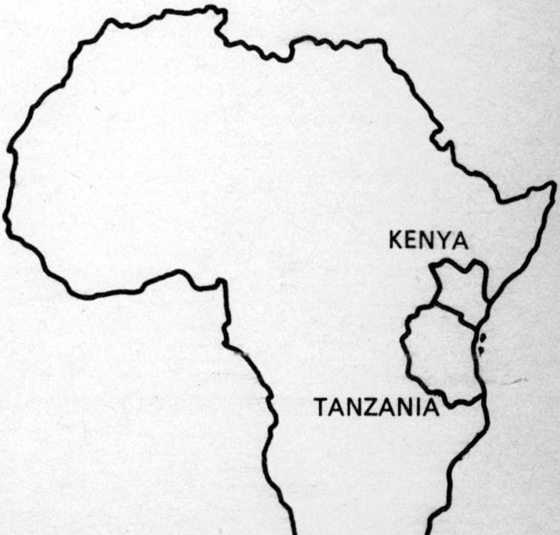

Travellers' guide to Kenya and Northern Tanzania

RICHARD COX

GEOGRAPHIA

Other titles in this series are:

Travellers' Guide to Egypt
Travellers' Guide to Portugal
Travellers' Guide to the South of France
Travellers' Guide to Greece
Travellers' Guide to Ireland
Travellers' Guide to Israel
Travellers' Guide to Malta, Gozo and Comino
Travellers' Guide to Southern Africa
Travellers' Guide to Majorca

Thornton Cox Travellers' Guides
Kenya and Northern Tanzania

First published 1984

Text by **RICHARD COX**
Drawings by **RENA FENNESSY**
Maps by **Tom Stalker-Miller, MSIA**

Geographia Limited
17–21 Conway Street
London W1P 6JD

Set in Univers by Input Typesetting Ltd, London SW19 8DR

Colour plates printed by Lithofast Co Ltd, Southend-on-Sea
Printed in Great Britain by The Guernsey Press Co Ltd, Guernsey, Channel Islands

0 09 207980 6

View of Mount Longonot across Lake Naivasha

Contents

Acknowledgements

The author gratefully acknowledges the assistance of many tour operators in Kenya, notably Abercrombie and Kent, Bunson Travel Service and the Pan African Travel Organisation, during research work for the compilation of this guide. The author also wishes to thank the Tanzania Tourist Corporation for their co-operation in providing information.

Foreword

A decade ago everything about safaris was new and exciting to people visiting Africa. Today the word *safari*, which in the Swahili language simply means journey, has become internationalised, epitomising adventure. So-called safari parks have sprung up throughout Europe, which are little more than open-air zoos, while mass tourism to Africa has developed to the point where the main package tour circuits are laden with herds of mini-buses. In consequence, more discriminating travellers increasingly try to plan their own itinerary, or at least get tour operators to book them into lesser known areas. This book is primarily written for such people and is the successor to our *Travellers Guide to East Africa*, originally published in 1966.

Geographically, Kenya and Tanzania are part of East Africa and, since animals and birds do not recognise national frontiers, and the region has its own characteristics, the area is still referred to as East Africa occasionally in the text. Overall, the backdrop of East Africa's scenery is of epic proportions and remarkable variety. It is bounded to the east by the Indian Ocean, where the dhows of Arabia ply down to Zanzibar, Dar es Salaam and beyond, and the coral lagoons and big game fishing rival the Bahamas. To the west it reaches inland 800 miles to the second deepest lake in the world, Lake Tanganyika, and includes Lake Victoria, the second largest. To the north lie the highlands of Ethopia, a 3,000-year-old state with ancient castles and rock-hewn churches.

Striking down through the centre of this area goes the Rift, the great valley of Africa, part of a geological fault in the earth's surface that runs from the USSR to Zimbabwe, and cuts the channel of the Red Sea on the way. In Kenya the Rift is 80 km (50 miles) across in places and 2,000 ft deep. Its bed is pitted with extinct volcanoes, while not far from it rise the two highest peaks in the African continent, Kenya and Kilimanjaro, both volcanic, both permanently topped with snow. Either of these may have been the original 'Mountains of the Moon' although the name and the legends now attach to a third snowcapped range, the Ruwenzori in Uganda, near the border of Zaire. Ice and frost are no rarity in other continents, but here they are made dramatic, and even frightening, by the incongruity of their existence above the vast, hot plains below.

Much of the recorded history of both Kenya and Tanzania centres on the coast. Ptolemy, the great geographer, wrote in the second century AD, about Mombasa under the name of Tonike, and the long white coral beaches of both countries, verged with palm trees, were familiar to Indian, Arab and Portuguese adventurers and traders. Until a hundred years ago, the principal trade was with Arabs and Muslim Persians (known as *Shirazi*), who sailed down in the dhows to exchange their cloth, beads and wooden chests, for ivory, rhino horn and spices. Indeed the dhows still sail down today, although the Arab sultanates of the coast are long extinct.

When the early European explorers trekked inland, they found a landscape of bewildering beauty, teeming with game. Today the plains of the Serengeti, which seem as wide as an ocean, are still the scene twice a year of the greatest game migration in the world, and giraffe and gazelle are still as familiar a sight as cattle, while the profusion of birdlife is as breathtaking as the landscape.

Despite the demand for land for African farmers, there is great awareness of the need to conserve the game. President Nyerere's *Arusha Manifesto of 1961* stated, 'Wildlife is an integral part of our resources and of our future livelihood and wellbeing'. Unhappily this sentiment has been shared, but not backed up, in other countries. Although instituting improvements, like charting the great annual migrations of game, the authorities failed to stop massive depredations by poachers. The effects of this were at last realised in the late 1970s and in Kenya, for example, both hunting and the sale of game trophies are banned. In 1979 Kenya also placed a complete ban on the export of sea shells. Heavy fines face poachers. Even so, the preservation of the natural heritage has needed outside help, most notably from the World Wildlife Fund, which has given generous assistance to the game departments concerned and to the development of parks and reserves, while the East African Wildlife Society has also contributed substantially to local conservation of wildlife and its habitat.

Finally, it should be explained that although surface and air communications within Kenya have improved considerably over recent years, with many tarmac roads and scheduled flights operating to the Masai Mara and to the coastal town of Lamu, the frontier with Tanzania remains closed to tourists. You can only cross by special permission from the Office of the President of Tanzania in Dar es Salaam. Thus while telephone communications between the two countries are easy, there are no scheduled transport services, either by local or foreign carriers. The effect of this closure by the Tanzanian authorities has been that each country has developed self-contained tourist circuits.

In Tanzania it has concentrated tourist development on the north, with visitors arriving at the Kilimanjaro airport. In Kenya it has led to the opening up of various magnificent areas, notably the Mara, Lake Baringo and Lake Bogoria (formerly Lake Hannington) and the south coast.

General Information

How to get there

By air
Both countries run their own national airlines, namely Kenya Airways and Air Tanzania, but there are no scheduled services connecting the two countries, since the border is closed. Kenya Airways operates international services to Nairobi and Mombasa from London (Heathrow), Athens, Copenhagen, Frankfurt, Paris, as well as from Cairo, Jeddah, Bombay, Karachi and other Middle Eastern and Asian capitals. Air Tanzania is developing an international network, with routes to Bombay, Dubai, Jeddah and London.

Some 36 international airlines operate to Nairobi, including Aeroflot, Air France, Air India, Alitalia, British Airways, Egyptian Airlines, Ethiopian Airlines, El-Al Israel Airlines, Iberia, Japan Airlines, KLM, Lufthansa, Olympic, PIA, Pan Am, Sabena, Scandinavian, Sudan Airways, Swissair, TWA, Varig and Zambia Airways. Many of these also serve Tanzania, but not via Nairobi.

Among the few airlines linking East and West Africa are Ethiopian Airlines, Nigeria Airways, Pan Am and Air Zaire.

The international airports are Nairobi (Jomo Kenyatta) and Mombasa (Moi International) in Kenya, and Kilimanjaro and Dar es Salaam in Tanzania. Customs facilities are also available for charter flights at Nairobi's Wilson Airport. The departure tax for international flights is Shs 80/ – in both Kenya and Tanzania.

It is not possible to quote fares sensibly. APEX excursion fares from Britain run as low as £350 sterling on scheduled services of Air Kenya and British Airways, which is less than half the standard return fare. APEX tickets can have validity from 14 days to one year. Charter flights have been hit by local regulations restricting the sale of tickets in local East African currencies. Overall it is wise to consult a travel agent. Remember that internal travel can be much cheaper if added on as additional sectors to an international ticket.

Both countries are liable to make possession of a return ticket a condition of entry for visitors.

Note that local currencies are not accepted for purchases on board aircraft and often not in airport duty free shops.

Many travel agencies in Britain, Germany, Scandinavia and the United States offer inclusive holidays in East Africa. In Britain, these include Thomas Cook & Son, Hickie Borman Grant & Co, Nilestar, Flamingo, Swan-Hellenic, Kuoni Travel Ltd, Lunn-Poly, Houlder Brothers, Ingham's and Lord Brothers, all in London; in the United States, Lindblad Travel Inc of Westport, Connecticut, Intrav in St Louis, and Percival Tours in Los Angeles.

By Sea

In recent years virtually all passenger traffic by sea has ceased. Even cargo ships rarely take passengers, and their schedules are anyway extremely unreliable.

Overland

Overland treks are arranged by a number of specialist firms, as well as often being organised privately. The normal route crosses the western Sahara to West Africa and goes through the Central African Republic and northern Zaire. It takes about three months and is governed by the rainy seasons encountered on the journey. You camp en route and it is vital to have an experienced leader. Two firms which organise trips are Encounter Overland Ltd (271 Old Brompton Road, London SW5, telephone 01–370 6845) who also take the Nile route to Nairobi via Egypt and the Sudan, and Trail Finders Ltd (46 Earls Court Road, London SW5, telephone 01–937 9631). Prices, including food, run from £1,025 to Nairobi and £1,450 to Dar es Salaam. Many trips continue on to South Africa, which adds four weeks to the journey.

Internal transport

Local Air Charters

There are several hundred airstrips in Kenya and Tanzania, including ones in all the national parks and most reserves. In consequence flying is an accepted way of getting about and, given that you go direct, can often rival car hire costs. Nairobi to the Mara Game Reserve, for example, is less than one hour by air against six hours by road.

The main air charter companies in Nairobi include Africair (telephone 501210), Air Kenya (telephone 510601), CMC Aviation (telephone 501221), Safari Air Services (telephone 501211) and Sunbird Aviation (telephone 501421), all at Wilson Airport. At Mombasa's Moi International Airport there are Coast Air (telephone 433320) and Cooper Skybird Air Charters (telephone 433246). Malindi Air Services (telephone Malindi 153) operate at Malindi and Lamu, and Pioneer Aviation operates from Lamu to Nairobi on a scheduled basis. Sunbird operates a daily service from Wilson to the Masai Mara Reserve. Additionally the Aero Club of East Africa operates from Wilson Airport and accepts qualified private pilots for membership, as well as giving flying training.

Flying costs (early 1983) in a twin-engine charter varied from Shs 16/- per mile for a 5-seat Cessna 310 to Shs 26/- per mile for a 10-seat plane; ie Shs 2/60 per mile, per person. Single engine aircraft are cheaper. Self-fly rates start at around Shs 500/- per hour for a Cessna 150 to Shs 1,200/- per hour for a Cessna 182. Most air charter companies will rent-out aircraft to qualified pilots, but a Kenya licence is now required.

In Tanzania charter firms include Tanzanair, Tanzania Aviation Ltd, and Flight Service International, operating from Dar es Salaam and from Arusha.

Although the Tanzania – Kenya frontier is officially closed, charter flights are sometimes admitted by the Tanzanian authorities. Application has to be made to the Office of the President, State House, Dar es Salaam. There are no restrictions at the Kenyan end.

Car Hire and Driving
Avis and Hertz are both represented in Kenya, which means you can book through their international reservation systems. But there are reliable cheaper local firms. For fuller information, please refer to the Transport and Safaris sections of the Kenya and Tanzania chapters.

You drive on the left and you can use a current licence from your home country for up to 90 days. Both countries have speed limits: 88 kph (55mph) in Tanzania; 100 kph (62 mph) in Kenya. Distances are measured in kilometres.

Accommodation

Each country has its own system of classification. Please refer to the sections on Hotels and Game Lodges in the Kenya and Tanzania chapters. There are an increasing number of very cheap hotels, offering basic facilities which are not up to normal European standards but are perfectly adequate if you do not mind roughing it. There are also excellent youth hostels in many towns.

Altitude and Climate

Being on the Equator most of East Africa has no summer or winter and the days vary little in length. Sunrise is between 06.00 and 06.30 and sunset between 18.30 and 19.00. The sun rises and sets much faster than in temperate latitudes.

The climate is warm throughout the year, varying according to the altitude above sea level of the place you are at. At the coast daytime temperatures average between 75°F and 85°F (24°C and 29°C) with an average humidity of 75 percent. If there is no wind it can feel decidedly sticky, though at night it can be cool enough to wear a light pullover. Inland the humidity declines as you go higher up, and the nights become appreciably cooler. At 5,000 ft the average daytime temperatures are only slightly less than the coast's, but at night they fall to around 50°F (10°C). In the mountains the temperature drops to freezing point.

The sun is often hotter than it feels and you can all too easily get sunburnt, or find yourself suffering from heat exhaustion. In this climate your body needs more liquid than it does in temperate latitudes, which means drinking more, though not necessarily more alcohol! It is sensible to take water with you when driving a long distance. Finally, the sunlight is strong and you need good-quality sunglasses to protect your eyes.

Rain usually comes down in short downpours, after which the sun comes out again. Broadly speaking the long rains come to Kenya, and Northern Tanzania in April/May and the short rains in November and early December. However, in recent years the rainy seasons have been disobligingly erratic, so do not be surprised if you find it raining at some other time.

Complaints

If you have a complaint about a hotel or restaurant, address it to the Kenya Association of Hotelkeepers and Caterers (Box 44365 Nairobi, telephone 26027). Equally the Kenya Association of Tour Operators (Box 48461 Nairobi, telephone 29441) can help with safari or car rental problems. You could also approach the Ministry of Tourism (Box 30027 Nairobi, telephone 331030).

In Tanzania contact the Tanzania Tourist Corporation (Box 2485 Dar es Salaam, telephone 27671).

Currency and Banking

Kenya and Tanzania, each issue their own shillings as the basic unit. The shilling is a silver coloured round coin, divided into 100 cents. Lesser coins of ten and five cents are made of brassy yellow metal. Notes come in denominations of Shs 5/-, Shs 10/-, Shs 20/- and Shs 100/-. Theoretically these currencies are at par, but since the amounts one is allowed to take out are limited to Shs 100/- in Kenya and Shs 40/- in Tanzania, this question hardly arises. Nor do their international exchange ratios stay constant. The Kenya shilling is the strongest currency and at the time of writing was at Shs 20/60 to the £ sterling, Shs 12/74 to the US $ and Shs 5/36 to the DM. Large amounts are commonly expressed in pounds, with 20 shillings making £1.

Both countries have strict currency regulations, requiring a customs declaration to be completed on arrival. This form must be filled in and stamped by any hotel or bank which changes your money. It is then handed in to the customs on departure, though not always checked. Inevitably there is a considerable black market in both currencies and tourists are frequently accosted by touts on the streets. Quite apart from such men being adept at cheating by handing over the 'currency' in an envelope containing only ordinary paper, there are severe penalties if you are caught infringing the currency regulations and your passport will be impounded until after trial. Unspent foreign currency can, of course, be taken out.

Banking hours in Kenya are from 09.00 to 14.00 Mondays to Fridays and 09.00 to 11.00 on the first and last Saturdays of the month. Airport banks are open round the clock. Most hotels will change currency and travellers cheques. The principal banks are Barclays Bank International, Kenya Commercial Bank, Commercial Bank of Africa and the Standard Bank Ltd.

In Tanzania banking hours are 08.30 to 12.00 Monday to Friday and 08.30 to 11.00 on Saturdays. Banking facilities are provided by the National Bank of Commerce. Hotels are authorised to change foreign currency.

Customs Duties

Visitors are allowed to bring in duty free all bona fide personal effects, provided they are declared on arrival and the proposed stay is not over six months. This includes cameras, binoculars, portable typewriters; one bottle of spirits or perfumes; 50 cigars, or 200 cigarettes or ½ lb tobacco.

On certain articles a customs deposit can be demanded which is refunded on departure from East Africa. Motor vehicles covered by a triptique or carnet will be allowed duty free for the period of validity of the document.

Items that the customs tend to pounce on include transistor radios and tape recorders, though if they are demonstrably personal property they are normally let through. Gifts or anything intended for sale or exchange are liable to duty. Guns and ammunition must be declared, and need a firearms certificate from the police which safari organisers can obtain for you in advance.

Almost anything that is posted to you while you are in East Africa will have duty levied on it, usually at 30 percent of the estimated value, while some items like perfume attract 100 percent duty. Even personal clothing has to be visibly used to escape duty if it comes by post. It is preferable to send one's belongings by air freight.

The sale of game trophies is illegal in Kenya, with very rare exceptions. In Tanzania their sale is legal, since hunting is permitted. However in both countries the main restriction when you leave is on taking out hides, skins and ivory. Anything made from game animals, from zebra-decorated sandals to a whole mounted leopard skin, must have a Game Department Certificate, which shops should provide for you at the time of purchase. This is to prevent the sale and export of illegally trapped animal skins.

Diplomatic Representation

There are Kenyan diplomatic missions in Addis Ababa, Beijing, Bonn, Brussels, Cairo, Jeddah, Kinshasa, Lagos, Lusaka, London, Mogadishu, Moscow, New Delhi, Ottawa, Paris, Rome, Stockholm, Tokyo, Vienna and Washington. Visas or Visitor's Passes can be obtained from them (see Immigration below).

Over 60 countries maintain embassies or consulates in Nairobi, including Australia, Austria, Belgium, Brazil, Bulgaria, Canada, People's Republic of China, Colombia, Cyprus, Czechoslovakia, Denmark, Ethiopia, Finland, France, German Federal Republic, Ghana, Great Britain, Greece, Hungary, India, Iran, Ireland, Italy, Japan, Korean Republic, Kuwait, Lesotho, Liberia, Malagasy Republic, Malasia, Malawi, Netherlands, Nigeria, Norway, Pakistan, Poland, Rumania, Rwanda, Somalia, Spain, Sri Lanka, Sudan, Sweden, Switzerland, Swaziland, Thailand, Turkey, UAR, USA, USSR, Yugoslavia, Zaire and Zambia.

Belgium, Canada, France, India, Italy, The Netherlands and Sweden maintain consulates in Mombasa.

A growing number of international organisations have offices in Nairobi, including UNEP, which has its headquarters just outside the city, UNDP, UNESCO, UNICEF, FAO and the EEC.

There is no Tanzanian or Ugandan diplomatic represention in Nairobi, nor does Kenya have missions in those countries.

Tanzania has diplomatic missions in Addis Ababa, Basle, Beijing, Bonn, Brussels, Cairo, Conakry, The Hague, Harare, Khartoum, Kigali, Kinshasa, Lagos, London, Luanda, Lusaka, Maputo, Moscow, New Delhi, Ottawa, Paris, Rome, Stockholm, Tokyo, Washington and the United Nations.

Countries which maintain embassies or consulates in Tanzania, where the capital is due to be transferred from Dar es Salaam to Dodoma in the late 1980s, include Algeria, Angola, Australia, Austria, Belgium, Burundi, Canada, People's Republic of China, Cuba, Czechoslovakia, Denmark, Ethiopia, Finland, France, German Federal Republic, Great Britain, Guinea, Hungary, India, Indonesia, Israel, Italy, Ivory Coast, Japan (resident Nairobi), Korean Republic, Morocco, Netherlands, Nigeria, Pakistan, Romania, Rwanda, Somali Republic, Sweden, Switzerland, Turkey, UAR, USA, USSR, Yugoslavia, Zaire, Zambia.

Dress and Cosmetics

Comfortable clothes matter a lot, as in all tropical climates. For women a woollen jumper or cardigan is essential and a light woollen suit an asset. At the coast during the day light cottons and linens are the thing, preferably washable, and slacks and shirts for safaris. Sandals can be bought in holiday centres. Swimsuits and beachwear are useful. So are one pair of flattish shoes, and a raincoat, preferably a lightweight one. Sunglasses and a sunhat (obtainable locally) are all but vital.

For men a lightweight suit is useful in the cities. Bring plenty of shirts – incidentally in our experience synthetic fabrics can become very sticky and there is no substitute for cotton if you want to stay cool. A pair of washable trousers will be handy and so will both long- and short-sleeved sweaters.

East African hotels and clubs are not excessively formal and a dinner jacket is rarely needed. White tuxedos are less often worn than black ones. In general a dark light- to medium-weight lounge suit for a man, and a smart dress for a woman, will be enough for formal occasions, even if you are at a gathering when the African leaders are in national dress. This latter incidentally is both dignified and colourful. Tanzania's is reminiscent of the Roman toga.

Anyone going on safari will need neutral-coloured clothes so as not to alert animals to their presence. Jungle green or khaki bush shirts, trousers and skirts can be made locally, or bought off the peg. You will look right in them and they will be cheaper both in tailoring charges and air freight than any similar clothes you bring with you.

Quite a number of internationally known beauty preparations are sold in the cities. Sun lotions and moisturising creams are vital in this climate, though they are expensive. Equally razor blades, shaving soaps etc are available. Most hotels have plug sockets for electric razors in their bathrooms.

Electricity

The electricity supply in East Africa is 240 volts, 50 cycles, AC. Most hotels provide adaptor plugs for 220 volt and 110 volt appliances.

Etiquette

In general the welcome you get in Africa is refreshing, and Africans will often stop to talk to the foreign visitor. They are relaxed and informal people. It's fair to say, however, that they are sensitive on several points, notably religion, colonialism and photography.

Both Kenya and Tanzania have Moslem communities. Their mosques can be visited but it is best to ask the guardian of the mosque if you may venture inside. Before going in you must remove your shoes and please be fully dressed in all other respects.

While politics do not impinge on the visitor at all, do remember that these countries have only recently become independent of British rule and dislike rude remarks about their newly won freedom. The old habit of addressing servants and waiters as 'boy' has gone for ever. Some restaurants and hotels give their staff lapel name badges. In Tanzania one officially approved word for calling for service is *Rafiki* – the Swahili for 'friend'. Otherwise call out 'Steward' or 'Waiter'. Using occasional Swahili words (see page 18) will pay dividends in terms of service, even if you only learn *Jambo* and *Asante sana*. Some Africans, especially Moslems, do not like being photographed. It is often believed that by taking a picture of a man you gain control over his soul. If there is obvious hostility then be sensible and put your camera away, or ask the person concerned for his or her agreement. This may lead to a demand for money – in areas near Amboseli for example, to outrageous demands. A few shillings should normally be enough.

Food

In hotels and restaurants, in both Kenya and Tanzania, the cooking is basically English, with standard 'international' grills, roasts and other dishes. There are Chinese, French, Indian and Italian restaurants in the cities. In country towns menus are more basic. There is plentiful use of local fruit – such as avocado pears, bananas, mangoes, oranges, paw-paws and pineapples. In Kenya, beef, lamb and pork are abundant and fish is readily available: Nile perch, tilapia and trout from fresh water lakes and rivers, seafish, lobster and prawns from the coast. Kenya cheeses include locally made camembert, cheddar and gouda.

Until recently hotel menus did not include indigenous African foods or cooking. However these are increasingly being put on offer. Some of the ingredients and dishes with their Swahili names in italics, are as follows:

Samaki	fish, of any kind
Nyama	meat
Kuku	chicken
Pilao	Indian style rice with meat or vegetables
Githeri	beans and maize cooked together whole
Irio	beans or peas and maize and sometimes potatoes boiled together, seasoned and mashed
Matoke	plaintain bananas steamed, sometimes with coconut sauce
Mseto	boiled lentils and rice with onions, coconut and milk
Ndizi	plantain bananas (*matoke*) fried with onions
Sukuma wiki	a hard variety of spinach, boiled and mixed with whatever leftovers are available. The name means 'make the week last', it's a standby when money is running out
Ugali	a very thick maize porridge. Often eaten as the accompaniment to meat or stew

At the coast Swahili cooking, influenced by Arabian traditions, utilises exotic spices and coconut milk, often with grilled fish.

Additionally various Indian specialities have become widely adopted, for instance *samosas* which are small triangles of crisp pastry filled with minced meat and vegetables, and curries.

If you want to know about Kenyan menus, look for Kathy Eldon's book *Tastes of Kenya* published by Kenway Publications, Nairobi.

Drink

Local beers are lager style and a normal bottle is enough to fill two large glasses. The fixed price is Shs 6/70 a bottle. White Cap and Tusker are the most popular brands. Tusker Export and Tusker Premium are superior brews sold in smaller bottles at a slightly higher price. Guinness Stout is also brewed locally.

Soft drinks are also price controlled. Coca Cola, Fanta, Sprite and local lemonades are sold everywhere and are very cheap. Spirits are expensive, the best bargains being gin and vodka which are distilled locally. There are also local whiskies and brandies, created by mixing local and imported spirit. Scotch whisky costs whatever the shop thinks it can charge. At the time of writing this was never less than Shs 250/- and likely to rise. In Tanzania spirits are seldom available (see Tanzania chapter, page 116).

Wine is also expensive and not always available. Italian wines appear to travel best, but even they can suffer from secondary fermentation during shipment from Europe. Kenya Wine Agencies have developed a local white Riesling style wine made from paw paw juice, called 'Papaya'. This costs around Shs 30/- and is drinkable if properly chilled. In Tanzania there are other heavy rosé and red wines produced from a vineyard at Dodoma.

Normal bar opening hours in Kenya are 11.00 to 14.00 and 17.00 to 23.00. In Tanzania the hours are from 12.00 to 14.00 and 17.00 to midnight.

Water
Tap water is normally drinkable, though in some areas it is naturally highly fluorine and not suitable for pregnant women or young children. When it is not, hotels leave a Thermos flask of cold drinking water in your room.

Cigarettes
Locally made Kenyan cigarettes include Crown Bird Filter, a mild brand, Sportsman, which is stronger, and Embassy, the closest to an ordinary Virginia type. The tar content of cigarettes is not officially controlled.

Gratuities

Sometimes these are added to hotel and restaurant bills. Otherwise about 10 percent of the bill is fair, or 15 percent if you have had especially good service. Shs 2/- is normal for a luggage porter and Shs 5/- for the room servant after one or two nights, depending on how helpful he has been. If you are staying in a private house then Shs 10/- per day for each servant is appropriate. Drivers should be given around Shs 15/- per day and game rangers the same after a game drive.

Health

Officially if you are coming from Europe or other countries where such diseases as cholera are not endemic, you no longer require international certificates of vaccination against smallpox and inoculation against yellow fever. In practice, it is extremely unwise not to be immunised against yellow fever, cholera and typhoid; equally it is wise to take anti-malarial pills, starting before you arrive, even though up-country areas are not malarial. Nivaquin, Paludrine and Sensida are among the best anti-malarial tablets. These can be bought locally.

There are chemists' shops throughout East Africa, experienced doctors practise in most towns and there are good hospitals in the cities.

Do not swim in the inland lakes and rivers unless you are told it is safe, since they are often infested with bilharzia (a disease carried by water snails). Beware of over-exposure to the sun, which can definitely be injurious.

The Flying Doctor Service (Box 30125 Nairobi telephone 501301) is based at Wilson Airport. Most tour operators subscribe to it and so their clients can be flown back from anywhere in Kenya to a medical centre. Alternatively visitors can obtain one month's temporary membership for only Shs 25/-. There is also a Flying Doctor service in Tanzania.

Immigration

Visitors to both Kenya and Tanzania must have a Visitor's Pass, which can normally be obtained on arrival, subject where necessary to the possession of a valid visa.

Kenya does not require visas from citizens of Denmark, Ethiopia, Italy, Norway, San Marino, Spain, Sweden, Turkey, Uruguay, West Germany and the British Commonwealth (except Australia, Nigeria, Sri Lanka and British passport holders of Bangladeshi, Indian or Pakistani origin). Visas can be obtained from the Kenyan embassies listed in the Diplomatic Representation section above, or from British embassies abroad. They should be applied for 30 days in advance. Visitor's Passes are granted for a maximum of three months, but can be extended by application to the Immigration Department, Bima House, Harambee Avenue, Nairobi (telephone 332110). Visitors are not allowed to accept work, either paid or unpaid.

Tanzania does not require visas from Commonwealth citizens. Visas can be obtained from Tanzanian diplomatic missions abroad or by direct application to the Principal Immigration Officer, Box 512, Dar es Salaam. Visitors Passes are granted at the main entry points to the country. As in Kenya, visitors are not permitted to accept employment.

Language

English is spoken widely and is the accepted language in the cities, hotels, restaurants etc. However, as well as numerous tribal languages, East Africa has its own lingua franca, called Swahili. This is the official language of Tanzania and has its origin at the coast. Although you can manage perfectly well without knowing any Swahili, the following words and phrases will be useful. Swahili Grammars are available in East African bookshops.

Hello – Jambo
How are you? – Habari
Goodbye – Kwaheri
Please – Tafadhali
Thank you – Asante
Thank you very much – Asante sana
Today – Leo
Tomorrow – Kesho
Lion – Simba
Quickly – Upesi
Slowly – Polepole
Food – Chakula
Tea – Chai
Coffee – Kahawa

Beer – English understood, or Tembo (lit: elephant) in Kenya
Argument, problem – Shauri
Hot – Moto
Cold – Baridi
One – Moja
Two – Mbili
Three – Tatu
Four – Ine
Five – Tano
Six – Sita
Seven – Saba
Eight – Nane
Nine – Tisa
Ten – Kumi

Where is the nearest garage?	Wapi garage karibu zaidi?
Is the road ahead passable?	Naweza pita njia mbele?
Where is the nearest police station?	Wapi stesheni polisi karibu?
Where is the nearest telephone?	Wapi simu karibu?
Where does this road lead to?	Njia hii inakwenda wapi?
Do you know anyone who speaks English?	Unajua mtu anayesem kiingereza?
I want a room for one night with a bath	Nataka nyumba na bafu pamoja kwa siku moja
What time is it?	Saa ngapi?
Where is the nearest doctor?	Wapi dokitari karibu?

Where is the nearest hospital?	Wapi hospitali karibu?
Where is the German/French/ Danish/English/Swedish/ American Consulate?	Wapi Consul ya Gerumani/ Faranza/Denmark/Ingereza/ Sueden/Marekani?
Please direct me to a good hotel	Wapi hoteli mzuri
How much?	Pesa ngapi?
What time will food be ready?	Chakula tayari saa ngapi?
I want a cold beer	Nataka tembo baridi.

Pronunciation is important but easy. Every letter must be sounded. The consonant 'G' is always hard like the G in 'got'; 'CH' and 'SH' have the same sounds as in English. There are no diphthongs; vowels are pronounced as shown below.

a is like the a	in 'father'
e is like the a	in 'say'
i is like the e	in 'be'
o is like the o	in 'hoe'
u is like the oo	in 'too'

Photography

The sunlight here is intense and you should allow a faster exposure than you would in Europe. The DIN, ASA and Weston meter settings recommended by film manufacturers are now for the minimum exposure, not the average, and so are just about right for East African conditions. However, where there is a lot of refracted light, as on the dazzling white sands of the coast or some of the open plains, you will need a still shorter exposure. A lens hood is invaluable, while an ultraviolet filter cuts down the effects of glare. It is advisable to buy film before you arrive as film is expensive locally.

Photographing game you are obviously unlikely to get close enough to take a meter reading off the animal itself, which will need a greater exposure than the landscape it is in. A good way to check is by taking a reading off a dull-coloured piece of clothing, remembering to take a reading in shade if the animal you are about to photograph is lying in the shade. When using a telephoto lens, especially one you have not used before, it is wise to open the aperture an extra half stop.

Photographing Africans, whose dark skins reflect very little light, you need to open the aperture by at least one stop (eg f8 to f5.6).

Or of course you can halve the shutter speed (eg from 1/250th down to 1/125th sec).

Finally, be careful how you use a camera (see under Etiquette above). Never, under any circumstances, photograph government buildings, military camps and vehicles, or airports. Kenya is otherwise liberal towards photographers. In Tanzania, however, it is unwise to use a camera anywhere outside the game parks. The editor of this book was arrested while revising it.

Posts, Telegraphs and Telephone

There are no house-to-house deliveries of mail, so all postal addresses are Post Office box numbers. In Kenya and Tanzania internal letters cost 50 cents. Overseas airletter forms cost Shs 2/-. Airmail letters cost Shs 3/50 for every 10 grammes weight to Europe and Shs 5/- to America. Postcards cost Shs 2/50 airmail to Europe and Shs 3/50 to America.

A local telephone call costs Shs 1/- . Trunk call charges vary with distance. Subscriber trunk dialling has recently been introduced between the major East African cities and towns but is overloaded, and there is a shortage of public call boxes. Some of the STD codes are:

Arusha 057, Dar es Salaam 051, Diani Beach 01261, Malindi 0123, Mombasa 011, Nairobi 02, Nanyuki 0176, Nyeri 071.

International calls can be booked in Kenya by dialling 0196. The minimum charge is for three minutes and to Britain is Shs 72/- and to America Shs 90/-.

Public Holidays

Kenyan public holidays, when banks, shops and government offices close, are Christmas Day, Boxing Day, New Year's Day, Good Friday, Easter Monday, Labour Day (May 1), Madaraka Day (June 1 or the following day if June 1 falls on a Sunday), Kenyatta Day (October 20), Jamhuri (Independence) Day (December 12). Additionally the Moslem holidays of Idd-ul-Fitr and Idd-ul-Haj are observed by all people of the Islamic Faith. (See Tanzania below.)

In Tanzania official public holidays, when government offices, banks and shops close, are Christmas Day, Zanzibar Revolution Day (January 12), CCM Day (February 5) Good Friday, Easter Monday, International Workers Day (May 1), Union Day (April 26), Maulid Day (mid-June), Farmers Day July 7, Independence and Republic Day (December 9), Idd-ul-Fitr, Idd-ul-Haj. These last two are Moslem religious festivals and the actual dates vary from year to year.

Security

Cities pose obvious dangers of theft. Do not carry large amounts of cash or valuables with you, especially not wallets in hip pockets. No matter where you are, do not leave money or travellers cheques in hotel rooms or in vehicles: indeed never leave anything of value in a vehicle, even out in the bush. Do not walk alone along deserted parts of the beach carrying valuables, whether cameras or rings or watches, and be careful in city streets at night. As far as crime in concerned, Tanzania is more secure than Kenya, though the dangers are less than they would be in central London or New York.

Shopping

Shopping in Kenya and Tanzania can broadly be divided into three kinds: first there are the European type products you need on safari, like film and suncream; secondly souvenirs; and thirdly artefacts which are works of art, as opposed to the mass produced souvenirs.

In the first category, toiletries, medicines, camera film and clothing are all easily available in Kenyan tourist centres and cities, though they are expensive by comparison to Europe or the USA. In Tanzania they are in very short supply. In either case, it is advisable to stock up before you come out, with the one exception that safari clothing is not expensive in Kenya and it is much easier to buy suitable bush jackets, hats and boots there than abroad. The Bata Shoe Company manufactures suede ankle boots and shoes which are hard wearing, comfortable and cheap at around Shs 260/- a pair. There are Bata stockists all over Kenya. It is also easy to get wildlife reference books.

Mass production sounds an odd word to apply to African souvenirs. However the handcarved stools, figurines, heads, animals, flywhisks, boxes, woven baskets, decorated gourds, copper bracelets and 'primitive' paintings which you see everywhere are turned out in huge quantities, albeit handmade because labour is cheaper in Africa than machinery. Among the best buys are baskets, ebony salad spoons, Arab inlaid boxes and the work of the Makonde carvers of Tanzania. Items not specifically made for tourists – like the baskets – include various kinds of cloth. There are Indian saris, African *kangas* (gaily printed lengths of cotton which make up well into summer dresses) and African *kikois* (a length of usually plain coloured cloth worn by men at the coast as a loincloth, but which can equally be made up). Both *kangas* and *kikois* are softer if they have been washed and cleaned; used ones can cost more than new ones. *Kikois* have a fringe which it is usual to tie into knotted strands. Always bargain over prices.

The third category of artefacts include the finer, individual, work of Makonde carvers, old African masks (if genuine), Ethiopian silver, old brass-bound and decorated chests, batiks by known African artists, soapstone ornaments and meerschaum pipes. The soapstone from Kisii in Kenya furnishes both mass produced articles of considerable vulgarity and fine work. Semi-precious stones are mined in both countries. Tanzanite is a sapphire-like blue stone. Tsavorite is a green garnet. Rubies are mined in Kenya and diamonds in Tanzania. Aquamarines, tourmalines, amethysts, and sapphires are available. But prices are seldom low. The names of jewellers and of shops specialising in African handcrafts are given in the text under the appropriate towns.

Shopping hours in Kenya are from 08.30 to 12.30 and 14.00 to 16.30 Mondays to Fridays and 08.30 to 12.30 on Saturdays. Officially shops are closed on Saturday afternoons and Sundays, but in practice many stay open part of the weekend in Nairobi. There are shops selling film, curios and so on at most game lodges.

In Tanzania shopping hours are from 07.30 to 12.30 and 14.00 to 18.00 on weekdays.

Sport

Golf, tennis, fishing, climbing, polo, racing, football and cricket are all widely available. The skin diving at the coast, called goggling locally, and the scuba diving are superb, and there is surfing, water-skiing and sailing.

Time

Local time in Kenya and Tanzania is three hours ahead of GMT. Thus in the European winter when it is midday (12.00) in Kenya it will be 09.00 in Britain and, allowing for the exact date of change to summer time, 10.00 in Europe. In summer, when BST is in force, it will be 10.00 in Britain and 11.00 in Europe when it is midday in Kenya. In New York the time will be 01.00 when it is midday in Kenya.

Weights and Measures

Kenya and Tanzania have converted to the metric system.

East Africa's Wildlife

If you want to know more, visit the wildlife exhibition in the Nairobi Museum and try the bibliography at the end of this section. Two handy guides are the *Shell Guide to East African Birds* and the *Shell Guild to Wildlife*, from which we are grateful for permission to reproduce some of these drawings by Rena Fennessy.

Animals

Here are some of the animals you are most likely to see on safari

Swahili names are given in italics

The **African Elephant**, *Ndovu* or *Tembo*, is larger than the Indian, particularly its ears. A bull weighs up to six tons and stands 12 ft at the shoulder. The heaviest recorded single tusk, from Tanzania, reached 228 lbs. Elephant are intelligent, live in herds and are vegetarians. They inhabit both the bush and the mountain forests. Their life span is about 60 years.

The **Hippopotamus**, *Kiboko*, whose name is Latin for 'river horse', is really of the pig family. Hippos congregate in 'schools' and spend most of the day submerged in water up to their nostrils. They come ashore to feed on grass at night. A grown hippo weighs two and a half tons, yet can outrun a man. Male hippos fight each other to the death.

The **African** or **Black Buffalo**, *Nyati* or *Mbogo*, has been forced to live in the forests and thick bush by encroaching civilisation, despite its basic food being grass. Buffalo stay in herds, and though shy are one of the most dangerous Big Game animals. A grown bull will weigh 1,500 lbs and the span of its horns may be 50 inches.

The **Black Rhinoceros**, *Faru*, weighs over a ton and is a solitary animal, fond of the thorn scrub. It has poor sight but good smell and hearing. Although a vegetarian, it is bad-tempered and will charge anything, even a train. The rare **White Rhino** (not illustrated) is larger and better tempered, but not white. Its name derives from the Dutch *weit*, meaning wide, which refers to its distinctive square jaw, The rhinos' horns are composed of tightly packed hair, not real horn.

The **Giraffe**, *Twiga*, the tallest mammal, grows to 18 ft and weighs half a ton. It browses on leaves, especially acacia, likes open country and is inoffensive. Its small horns are covered in skin and soft hair. The **Reticulated Giraffe** is so called because its markings are square, within a network of whitish lines, instead of star-shaped.

The **Common Zebra**, *Punda Milia*, is found in open country over most of Kenya and Tanzania, always managing to look sleek and well fed. Zebra move in herds, often with giraffe, eland and other animals. They feed on grass, leaves and, if necessary, shrubs. A male zebra stands five ft high at the shoulder and weighs 700 lbs. The rarer **Grevy's Zebra** is taller, has larger ears and narrower stripes.

The **Lion**, *Simba*, is found in open country throughout East Africa. A full-grown male weighs 400–500 lbs. The lioness has no mane. 'Prides', or families, of lion doze in the shade during the day and hunt at dusk, springing on the backs of the zebra, buffalo, wildebeest or whatever they have stalked. They kill only when hungry, once in three or four days.

The **Leopard**, *Chui*, hunts by night, is wary, and extremely dangerous when wounded or cornered. It makes its lair in cliffs, or among rocks in thick bush. Its favourite food is baboon, though if hungry it will eat rodents and even insects. A grown male weighs under 150 lbs. and measures about seven and a half ft from nose to tail.

The **Serval Cat**, *Mondo*, is short-tailed, long-legged and spotted, with large ears. It looks like a cross between a small leopard and a lynx. It hunts at night, feeding on birds and small mammals. The serval is widespread, particularly liking places that are marshy or near water.

The **Cheetah**, *Duma*, looks like a leopard, but with longer legs and smaller head. Also its spots are isolated, not grouped in a pattern. It hunts by day and is the fastest mammal in the world – it has been timed at 60 mph. Cheetahs stand three ft at the shoulder and are about seven ft long. They are easily tamed and have been raced against greyhounds in Europe.

The **Wart Hog**, *Ngiri*, is named after the warts on its grotesque head. It lives on the plains in families, or 'sounders', and breeds in holes. During the day it crops grass, or digs for roots with its tusks, while kneeling on its forelegs. It is related to the Giant Forest Hog, largest of the African pigs, which weighs over 300 lbs.

The **Spotted Hyena**, *Fisi*, is a night-time scavenger. Though its jaws can crush bones it is a coward and only attacks weak or aged animals. Its colour is yellowish and it weighs about 150 lbs. Hyenas have a characteristic, unpleasant howl and they 'laugh' when lions are around.

The **Baboon**, *Nyani Mkubwa*, is a large dog-faced monkey seen in many parts of East Africa. It lives on the ground, usually moving in troops under the leadership of a big old male, and goes into the trees to sleep at night. Baboons will eat practically anything, animal or vegetable. The babies ride on their mothers' backs.

The **Patas Monkey**, *Kima*, roams in troops of ten or 12, like the baboons. It normally stays on the ground, using low trees or anthills as observation points. Its habitat is the dry savannah of north-west Kenya and of Tanzania. In colour it is reddish, with white underparts and white side-whiskers on its face.

The **Lesser Bush Baby**, *Komba*, is a nocturnal relative of the monkeys, and lives mainly in acacia bush. Driving at night you often see its large eyes winking red at you out of the darkness. It is very active, climbing and making tremendous leaps in search of insects and fruit. During the day it sleeps, whole families cuddling together in hollow tree trunks.

Grant's Gazelle, *Swala Granti*, likes dry open grassland or even desert. It has graceful lyre-shaped horns, which both sexes carry, and is pale buff in colour, with a white rump and underside and a chestnut streak down the centre of the face. The male stands about 32 inches high at the shoulder. Gazelles are a species of antelope, with slender legs.

Thomson's Gazelle, *Swala Tomi*, known as the 'Tommy', is more reddish in colour than the Grant's Gazelle which otherwise it is like, and has a distinctive black band running along its flank. It also has a habit of twitching its small tail. The Tommy lives in large herds on the plains.

The **Gerenuk**, or Walter's Gazelle, *Swala Twiga*, has a delicately incongruous long neck and a giraffe-like head. It is a dark rufous colour, paler on the flanks, and with white bands over its eyes. It stands 36 to 41 inches high at the shoulder and weighs about 100 lbs. Only the males have horns. Gerenuk wander in small groups, browsing on leaves in acacia thorn country.

The **Dikdik**, *Dikidiki* or *Suguya*, stands only 15 inches high and weighs 12 lbs. It lives in the driest thorn scrub and is usually seen in pairs. In colour it is grey or grizzled brown, has a shaggy coat and a distinctively long nose. The **Klip-springer** is in many ways similar, but larger, standing about 21 inches high at the shoulder.

The **Uganda Kob**, of north-west Kenya, and Uganda, stands three ft high at the shoulder. It has a sleek red-gold coat, with white underparts and white rings round the eyes. The kob drinks daily, so is never far from water. It stays in herds and the males fight savagely to master their harems.

The **Impala**, *Swala Pala*, is a timid, medium-sized antelope, famous for leaping in the air when alarmed – it can jump 30 ft and rise ten ft above the ground. Impala move in large herds. They have smooth chestnut-coloured coats and tufts of black hair on the hind legs above the hooves. Only the males carry horns. Found in acacia bush and scrub country.

The **Common Waterbuck**, *Kuro*, is a large and handsome antelope found in eastern Kenya and Tanzania, usually near water. A bull may lead a herd of up to 30 cows, who have no horns. Their coats are shaggy, greyish brown, and with a white ring on the rump.

The **Sable Antelope**, *Palahala* or *Mbarapi*, is a splendid animal, standing nearly five ft high, almost black, and bearing great scimitar-shaped horns. It is white on the underparts, rump, and face. In East Africa it is only found in a few coastal areas of Tanzania, and near Mombasa in the Shimba hills. It likes lightly wooded country and stays in small herds.

The **Oryx**, *Choroa*, one of the most handsome, powerful and fierce antelopes, is found in varying species from Ethiopia to the Kalahari. It is reddish brown in colour, with black and white face markings. The female grows longer horns than the male – up to 40 inches. Oryx stand four ft high at the shoulder and weigh up to 450 lbs. They move in small herds. Amboseli and Tsavo are good places to look for them.

The **Greater Kudu**, *Kandala Mkubwa*, likes rocky and mountainous bush. A male stands five ft high at the shoulder and weighs about 600 lbs. The female has no horns. Kudus' bodies are a lavender grey colour, with white stripes. The **Lesser Kudu**, *Kandala Ndogo*, is rather smaller and has no fringe of hair running down its throat. It lives in thick bush and scrub.

Coke's Hartebeest, usually known as the *Kongoni*, is widely distributed in Kenya and Tanzania. It stays in large herds, grazing, while one animal acts as sentinel. When surprised it snorts, stamps a foreleg and gallops away. Its colour is light fawn, and its bracket-shaped horns and steeply sloping hindquarters make it easily recognisable.

The **Wildebeest** or **Gnu**, *Nyumbu*, seen in vast herds migrating across the Serengeti Plains every year, is one of the commonest antelopes in open country all over East Africa. It has a dark grey body, a white beard, a shaggy mane, and a clumsy gait. Its horns look slightly like a buffalo's. It stands about five ft high at the shoulder.

The **Eland**, *Pofu* or *Mbunja*, the largest of the antelopes, congregates in large herds, often alongside zebra and giraffe. They are found in open country in both Kenya and Tanzania. Both sexes carry heavy twisted horns. A full-grown bull weights over 1,050 lbs and stands six ft high at the shoulder. Their colour is greyish brown, with light stripes.

The **Ostrich**, one of the sights of Africa, cannot fly but has a kick than can kill a man and can run at 45 mph. Fully grown, it can be eight ft high. It lays eggs in clutches of 14 or more. You often see it on the plains among herds of animals. True to stories it does sometimes hide its head on the ground when approached.

Forest Animals

The **Bongo**, same name in Swahili, is the largest of the forest antelopes, though smaller than an eland. It stands four ft high at the shoulder and both sexes carry horns. In colour it is a bright reddish chestnut, with vertical white stripes. Bongo live only in the mountain forests, are very shy and seldom seen.

The **Bushbuck**, *Mbawala* or *Pongo*, is a beautifully marked small animal, with a white underside to its tail. It prefers forest thickets to open country, is shy, and lives in families, not herds. A male stands three ft high at the shoulder and weighs about 100 lbs. The **Sitatinga**, *Nzohe*, is a swamp-dwelling variant of the same species.

The **Colobus Monkey**, *Mbega*, is jet black in colour, with a magnificent white mantle round its back, a white face and a white-tipped bushy tail. It lives in highland forests, like the Aberdares of Kenya, eats leaves and very rarely descends from the trees.

Sykes Monkey, *Kima*, often called the Blue Monkey, is dark blue-grey in colour, with black forelimbs, hands, feet, crown of head and tip of tail, It eats fruit and greenery, and inhabits forests near water. It is known for its friendliness. Variants of the species are called Silver and Golden Monkeys, from their colouring.

Birds

Kenya and Tanzania shelter over 1,200 species of birds, if all the winter migrants coming from Europe are included, and bird watching will take you into some of the most fascinating areas. Most safari firms incorporate bird watching in their game viewing arrangements.

At the coast in March and April plovers and sandpipers migrate north en masse and there are always a multitude of waterbirds: curlews, white egrets, green backed herons, cormorants and others.

On the inland lakes you will find pelicans and storks and, of course, the million strong flocks of flamingoes which frequent the Rift Valley lakes of Bogoria, Nakuru and Natron, turning the shores pink.

In plains country you find everything from ungainly ostriches (see page 30) to the brilliantly coloured Paradise flycatcher, from lilac breasted rollers and tiny sunbirds to vultures and the long legged, snake eating, secretary bird. Even in Nairobi gardens there is a spectacular variety of birdlife.

Safaris

The glamourous international image of the safari was originally created back in the days before World War I when legendary hunters like Karamoja Bell and F. C. Selous roamed the plains after elephant, lion and the other three of the 'Big Five': leopard, buffalo and rhino. The great American sporting connection with East Africa began when President Theodore Roosevelt spent three months in Kenya in 1911, after his term of office. His famous safari set off from Nairobi's Norfolk Hotel with 100 African porters, all in blue sweaters, carrying everything needed in the bush from gifts to ammunition. A complete entourage of professional hunters went with him. This sporting tradition, which inspired Hemingway's *Green Hills of Africa* and many other novels, was carried on by hunters as diverse as Bill Ryan, who shot his first lion when he was 11, and Eric Rundgren – who once fought off and killed a leopard with his bare hands. Clients came from America and Europe for the modern equivalent of Roosevelt's safari: much shorter in time, with hunting cars and trucks instead of porters, and with sprung mattresses, refrigerators and two-way radio in the camps set up for them in the bush.

Today public awareness of the need for game conservation has greatly reduced the scope for hunting, which is totally banned in Kenya, though permitted in some areas of Tanzania. But the tradition of the field safari has died hard and those who can afford it still go out for photographic safaris in the old style, while a number of former professional hunters have originated specialist safaris, for example for bird watching, with camels and on horse-back. It remains true that only by pitching camp in the wild can you get the proper feel of Africa and only with patience and the aid of skilled African trackers can you learn how it feels to follow game on foot. To walk for a week through the bush, as the author has done, is to find a very different world from the minibus game viewing of the national parks: and his was a very short safari. The real minimum is ten to 14 days.

Hunting

In Tanzania hunting is under the control of the Wildlife Corporation and is principally allowed in the south of the country, as well as to the west of the Serengeti. Two American companies operating in conjunction with the Wildlife Corporation are Safari Outfitters Inc (85 Michigan Avenue, Chicago, IL 60603, telephone 312/346 9631) and International Big Game Safaris (100 South Waverly Road, Holland, Michigan 49423, telephone 616/392 6458). The Kenyan hunter, Alfredo Pelizzoli (Box 48287, Nairobi, telephone 891381) has a hunting concession in Tanzania, while in the country itself Dr von Nagy (Box 659 Arusha, telephone Usa River 43) has a unique concession to operate in the Mount Meru area, hunting in the traditional Hungarian way from hides. The cost of a field safari would be around US$550 per person per day for two exclusive of game licences. Trophies can be prepared and shipped from Arusha.

Photographic and Specialist

The most renowned firm operating in Kenya is Ker Downey Safaris Ltd (Box 41822, Nairobi, telephone 556466). One of the region's professional hunting firms for many decades, they turned to full scale photgraphic field safaris after hunting was banned in Kenya, though they can still arrange hunting in such other countries as Botswana and the Sudan. Abercrombie and Kent Ltd (Box 59749 Nairobi, telephone 334955) similarly arrange full scale camping safaris and also combine them with occasional nights in lodges. A smaller, very personally-run firm is Robert Lowis' Trans African Guides (Box 49538 Nairobi, telephone 891172). Lowis specialises in bird watching safaris. All three of these firms provide complete camp staff, tentage and vehicles. Costs are around US$250 per person per day for each of four people or US$175 if use is made of game lodges.

A slightly different operation, based on their own private lodge on a 1½ million acre game ranch on the Galana River (see page 93) is run by Galana Game and Ranching Safaris (Box 76 Malindi) who additionally have a private 6,500 acre ranch near Mount Kenya, again with a private lodge. Charges including guide and transport are around Shs 1,200/- per person per night. Another company using a base camp for foot safaris on a private ranch is Wilderness Trails, at Lewa Downs near Isiolo (booking agent Bataleur Safaris, Box 42562 Nairobi, telephone 27048). Lewa Downs is also the starting point for 6-day camel safaris run by Julian McKeand, a former game warden with unrivalled knowledge of the Samburu country (see also page 80). These cost Shs 4,300/- per person and can be booked through Flamingo Travel Ltd in the Hilton Hotel (Box 45070 Nairobi, telephone 27927).

Riding safaris have been developed over the past ten years by Safaris Unlimited Africa Ltd, (Box 20138 Nairobi, telephone 332132), whose rates for individually arranged camping safaris are around US$180 per day for each of four people. They have recently introduced a 5-day special riding safari based on the Mara River Camp, which runs from Monday to Saturday for only Shs 4,400/- plus Shs 1,100/- for transport by air or car to the Mara. Curiously, it is possible to get much closer to game on horseback than it is on foot.

Bibliography

Birds

The definitive reference book on birds is:
Birds of Eastern and North Eastern Africa by Mackworth Praed and C. H. B. Grant, published by Longmans in two volumes.
A handier reference book, easy to carry on safari is:
A Field Guide to the Birds of East Africa, by J. G. Williams and N. Arlott, published by Collins.
Birds of Africa by John Karmali, published by Collins is more of a coffee table book, though with superb photographs.

Butterflies

The definitive work is:
Butterflies of the Afrotropical region by Bernard D'Abrera, published by Lansdowne Editions. This is a large and comprehensive volume.
A Field Guide to the Butterflies of Africa by J. G. Williams, published by Collins, is a handy reference book.

Animals

There is a vast literature on game in Africa. A useful handbook for game watching is:
A Field Guide to the Larger Mammals of Africa by Jean Dorst and Pierre Dandelot, published by Collins.

For general reading we recommend the following, all of which were in print at the time of writing:
Born Free and *Living Free*, both about the lioness Elsa by the late Joy Adamson and published by Collins.
The Marsh Lions – the story of an African Pride by Brian Jackman and illustrated (with photographs and drawings) by Jonathan Scott and published by Collins. An excellent account of a group of lions, studied for two years in the Masai Mara.
Among the Elephants by Iain and Oria Douglas-Hamilton, published by Collins/Harvill. The world famous account of the elephants in Tanzania's Lake Manyara National Park.
Elephants at Sundown. The story of Billy Woodley by Dennis Holman, published by W. H. Allen. Account of a renowned Kenya game warden's conservation efforts.
The Enormous Zoo by Colin Willock, published by Longmans, Green.

Two classics which should be available in libraries are:
No Room in the Ark by Alan Moorehead, published by Cassell.
Serengeti Shall Not Die by Bernard Grzimek, published by Fontana.

General

A beautifully produced introduction to Kenya is:
The Book of Kenya by Gerald Cubitt and Eric Robins, published by Collins/Harvill.
The Cradle of Mankind by Mohammed Amin, published by Chatto and Windus is an illustrated account of the Samburu and Turkana people and the wildlife of Lake Turkana.

Vanishing Africa by Mirella Ricciardi, published by Collins is a deservedly best selling photographic essay on Kenya's tribes.
The Battle of the Bundu by Charles Miller, published by Purnell, describes the World War I campaigns of the great German General von Lettow-Vorbeck and the British attempts to defeat him in Tanganika.
Journey through Kenya by Mohammed Amin, Duncan Willetts and Brian Tetley, published by the Bodley Head. Magnificent colour photographs.
The Flame Trees of Thika by Elspeth Huxley, published by Penguin Books. Story of the authoress's childhood in Kenya.
Out of Africa by Karen von Blixen (Isak Dinesen) published by Random House New York. The classic about a Kenya farm in the 1920s.
Africa's Rift Valley by Collin Willock, published by Time-Life Books.

East African Wildlife Society

The Society's bookshop in the Hilton Hotel arcade, Nairobi, is an excellent place to buy wildlife literature and the Society's monthly magazine, SWARA, is an inexhaustible source of information on current wildlife topics and local developments. Back numbers are obtainable at the office.

Treetops – the hotel in a tree

Kenya

The Country

Kenya is a land of kaleidoscopic contrasts. Most visitor's first impressions are of the modern semi-skyscrapers of Nairobi, the sweeping Athi plains outside the city, and game straying among the thorn bushes of the Nairobi National Park. Going up-country, you will see the splendour of the Rift Valley, or pass coffee farms on the way towards the thick rain forests of the Aberdares, perhaps glimpsing the snow on the deceptively unimpressive peaks of Mount Kenya. These mountain forests harbour elephant, rhino, buffalo and that elusive antelope, the bongo. Beyond Mount Kenya lie the vast semi-deserts of the north, the magnificent Samburu and Turkana peoples and the 'jade sea' of Lake Turkana. The 'up country' landscapes, are one of the great attractions of Kenya. The other is the coast, with its perfect white coral beaches, Arab traditions and resort hotels. It is not surprising that Kenya fires the imagination of everyone who goes there and that in the two decades since Independence in 1963 it has become internationally recognised as one of the most magnificent and exciting holiday areas anywhere.

Geographically the country covers 582,647 sq km (225,000 sq miles) and lies across the Equator. Its Indian Ocean coastline is 608 km (380 miles) long, while its centre is cut by the Great Rift Valley, running north to south and containing a variety of lakes. The largest river is the Tana, which flows in a wide curve eastwards from the slopes of Mount Kenya (17,058 ft) to the Indian Ocean. The climate is described in the General Information section.

Historically more has been discovered about Kenya in the years since Independence than ever before. The earliest inhabitants left no written records and Independence has generated keen interest in the country's heritage. Recent investigations by Richard Leakey, Director of the Nairobi Museum, and others have revealed fossilised remains of hominids at Koobi Fora on the eastern shore of Lake Turkana which are approximately 3 million years old: these bones of early men are so old that they suggest Kenya was the cradle of mankind. There are also a variety of hand-axe, or Acheulean sites dating from 1.4 million years ago to 150,000 years ago, which show the continuity of human descent in this part of Africa.

However, the present African population owes its origin to far more recent migrations: of Cushites from the north some 9,000 years back whose descendants are still nomadic; of Bantu from the west 1,000 years ago; and of Nilotics from what is now the Sudan, some 400 years ago. The earlier inhabitants survive in only three tiny groups: the Ndorobo of the forests, the Boni and the Sanye.

Today Kenya is home to Arabs, Asians and Europeans as well as more than 48 main African tribes. Some, like the Masai, are famous as warriors. Others, like the El Molo up at Lake Turkana (Rudolf) or the Waliangulu elephant hunters near Tsavo Park, are few in number, shy and still backward. The largest are the Kikuyu (3.2 million), whose homelands are between Nairobi and Nyeri, followed by the Luya (2.1 million) of the Kisumu area on Lake Victoria and the Kamba (1.75 million) centred on Machakos and Kitui. President Daniel arap Moi comes from the small Kalenjin tribe of western Kenya. The total population is nearly 17 million. A century ago there was great rivalry between the tribes, but today everything is concentrated on collaboration and Kenya's motto is *Harambee*, which means 'Let's all pull together'.

Nonetheless traditional dances and costumes are cherished as part of the country's cultural heritage. Their innate vitality always impresses, and the Chuka drummers, for instance, have drawn crowds to overseas performances in London and elsewhere. Broadly-speaking, there are two ways of getting to see traditional dancing. First if there is a celebration on, such as Independence Day (December 12), there are likely to be public performances. Secondly, if you are on a tour, you may find an exhibition arranged at some point, for instance at Bomas of Kenya in Langata outside Nairobi or Mayer's Ranch near Kijabe in the Rift Valley. Many hotels have performances – indeed the fierce dancer wielding a spear may be the same man who earlier carried your suitcase to your room! One word of warning here. If you happen accidentally upon a local *ngoma*, which is Swahili for a dance or celebration, make sure to ask if you may stay and watch, especially before taking photographs. These are private affairs.

Equally, if you want to see a representative selection of traditional huts, implements and crafts you should visit the Bomas of Kenya.

When the British colonised and developed Kenya they introduced both Asian and European minorities. The Asians came mostly to work on the railway, then branched into trade. Since Independence many have left and there are now about 50,000 of them, mainly in the cities, and you will notice their mosques, temples and bazaars, the Sikhs' turbans, and the women's brightly coloured saris.

The European settlers have progressively been replaced by African farmers. However, their influence remains evident both socially and in business, reinforced by a large influx of businessmen and officials from many international agencies. The European population is about 40,000. Down at the coast there is a sizeable Arab community.

Independence day was on December 12, 1963, and a year later Kenya became a Republic in the Commonwealth, under the Presidency of Mzee Jomo Kenyatta (*Mzee* is an honorific title, roughly translatable as 'wise old man'). He died in 1978 and his successor is the Hon Daniel arap Moi. The National Assembly sits in Nairobi. Administratively Kenya is divided into seven provinces – The Coast, Rift Valley, Central, Nyanza, Western, Eastern and North Eastern.

A glance at the map shows that Nairobi is at the centre of a spider's web of communications, with roads that have been enormously improved in recent years. To the west and north west, road and rail lead to the Rift Valley, Lakes Naivasha and Nakuru, then over the Mau Summit to Kisumu and Lake Victoria. Branching from the main road is one to Narok and the Masai Mara Game Reserve. North, both road and rail run along the eastern side of the Aberdare Mountains to Nyeri and Nanyuki, passing the vast bulk of Mount Kenya. The railway stops at Nanyuki, but the road goes on to descend the dramatic escarpment to Isiolo and the vast semi-desert of the North Eastern Province – the Northern Frontier District of former days – with the 'jade sea' of Lake Turkana. South east, road and rail march side by side to Mombasa and the coast via the Tsavo Park, while directly south is the road through Masailand to Arusha in Tanzania. For convenience we will divide Kenya into the areas to which these major routes lead, but dealing first with the national parks and game reserves and with the capital city itself.

Hotels and Game Lodges

In recent years Kenya's tourist facilities have been enormously improved, both in the number and quality of hotels and in the roads that serve them. The coast, especially around Mombasa and Diani Beach, has seen great expansion and the demand for accommodation in or near the national parks has led to a number of first class tented camps being established. At the other end of the scale, there is a good chain of youth hostels which charge only Shs 20/- a night and a large number of cheap, basic hotels, which cater equally for less well off African travellers and overseas visitors. Thus the range of facilities is now far wider than it was ten years ago, and we only mention establishments in the text which can be recommended relative to their status.

In 1983 the Kenya Association of Hotelkeepers and Caterers (Box 44365 Nairobi) initiated a classification system for hotels, lodges and camps and we give the appropriate grading in brackets after each hotel. (You will find individual hotels mentioned in the sections dealing with each region.) Their list is divided between town/business hotels, vacation hotels and lodges. As mentioned under Complaints in the General Information section, the Association will assist if you have a complaint against any of its member establishments.

The approximate price range of hotels in each grade was as follows during the 1983 high season, including government taxes. The peak season is January to March and you should expect at least a 10 percent price rise each year. In the low season of April to mid-July most coast hotels, lodges and camps offer substantial discounts.

Hotels:	**Town and Business**	
Class A	Double, room only	Shs 700/- to Shs 880/-
	Single, room only	Shs 480/- to Shs 710/-
Class B	Double, with breakfast	Shs 450/- to Shs 580/-
	Single, with breakfast	Shs 280/- to Shs 415/-
Class C	Double, with breakfast	Shs 400/- to Shs 625/-
	Single, with breakfast	Shs 290/- to Shs 425/-
Class D	Double, with breakfast	Shs 210/- to Shs 290/-
	Single, with breakfast	Shs 110/- to Shs 210/-
Class E	Some 30 very cheap hotels come into this category which we only mention when there is no other hotel in the town.	

Hotels:	**Vacation**	
Class A	Double, full board	Shs 900/- to Shs 1,600/-

Class A	Single, full board	Shs 530/- to Shs 1,014/-
Class B	Double, full board	Shs 850/- to Shs 1,050/-
	Single, full board	Shs 580/- to Shs 660/-
Class C	Double, full board	Shs 580/- to Shs 765/-
	Single, full board	Shs 375/- to Shs 600/-
Class D	Double, full board	Shs 470/- to Shs 600/-
	Single, full board	Shs 285/- to Shs 450/-
Class E	Double, full board	around Shs 440/-
	Single, full board	around Shs 280/-

Most of the coastal hotels are basically package tour hotels. Many only quote prices on application. Bed and breakfast or half board terms are not always available.

Lodges

Class A	Double, full board	Shs 900/- to Shs 1,150/-
	Single, full board	Shs 660/- to Shs 880/-
Class B	Double, full board	Shs 686/- to Shs 900/-
	Single, full board	Shs 482/- to Shs 650/-
Class C	Double, full board	Shs 550/- to Shs 660/-
	Single, full board	around Shs 420/-

Note that lodge (and tented camp) prices may seem high compared to their grading, but they are invariably in remote places where the costs of supplies and administration are high. Lodges which are called 'clubs' by their owners are usually not granted a classification, even though visitors can be freely booked in by travel agents.

Tented Camps

Class A	Double, full board	Shs 735/- to Shs 985/-
	Single, full board	Shs 450/- to Shs 677/-
Class B	Prices are little less than for Class A	

General Advice

In Kenyan hotels the standard check out time is 10.00. Double rooms are normally twin-bedded, and triple rooms are generally available. You should note that while hotels offer broadly international standards, accommodation in the wild is of necessity different. Lodges and camps are usually sited so as not to interfere with the natural surroundings, using local stone and timber. Rooms tend to be small and simply furnished, though comfortable, with private toilet facilities. Tented camps normally provide full-sized beds in insect-proofed tents, often with private showers and toilets. The forest lodges, often called 'tree hotels', are effectively luxury game lookouts, operated in conjunction with base hotels; thus Treetops in the Aberdares works in conjunction with the Outspan Hotel in Nyeri. Rooms in the tree hotels are very small and you should only take a small overnight bag with you. Self-help lodges usually have basic furnishings and a stove, but you have to bring your own food and there is no service. They are mainly used by local residents.

Lodges and camps – except the self-help ones – have restaurant and bar facilities, normally with a set menu. The larger ones have swimming pools. There is seldom any organised entertainment apart from game drives, which on average cost Shs 600/- to Shs 700/- for a vehicle for a morning or afternoon. Remember that you are out in the wild and it is dangerous to wander away from the lodge unescorted.

National Parks and Reserves

These are the two kinds of area in which game is protected and facilities are maintained for visitors to see and enjoy it. There are some 39 of them. All have roads and most have airstrips and are open throughout the year, except for the mountain parks, which may be inaccessible in wet weather. Entrance fees are Shs 30/- per person and Shs 30/- per car or light aircraft except where otherwise stated. Season tickets are available to Kenya residents. The gates are open approximately from dawn to dusk and regulations include a ban on travel at night – you must then be either out of the park or at a game lodge. You can only move about by vehicle and the speed limit is 20 mph, which is commonsense because you see nothing if you hurry. Nor may you leave the vehicle except at clearly indicated places, again commonsense because big game, though often used to cars, are still dangerous. Indeed, animals are less shy of cars than of human beings. There are no restrictions on amateur photography, but professional work requires a licence. The parks are run by the Wildlife Conservation and Management Department of the Ministry of Tourism and Wildlife. The Department's HQ is on the Langata Road, near the entrance to the Nairobi National Park (Box 40241 Nairobi, telephone 891601). Each park has wardens and a staff of rangers. These rangers wear green uniforms and sometimes a Foreign Legion type of hat. National reserves are run by local authorities on similar lines with game scouts, though (unlike the national parks) the indigenous tribes continue to live in them. Forest reserves are simply areas of planned afforestation.

Although the game lodges all have special booking agents, listed as they occur in the text, any travel agent can make your reservations. Camping is allowed at designated sites in most parks.

The increasing awareness of the need to protect special habitats and flora as well as fauna – not to mention tropical fish and coral – has led to the establishment of many new parks. A complete list is in the index, and all are mentioned in the text. Among the best known are:

Amboseli National Park
380 sq km (147 sq miles) of swamps and plains country inside a 3,260 sq km reserve, dominated by the snowcapped peak of Kilimanjaro. About 3,500 ft above sea level. See pages 85–87.

Masai Mara Game Reserve
1,813 sq km (700 sq miles) round the Mara River in SW Kenya. Mostly 5,000 ft up. One of the best parts of Kenya in which to see plains game. See pages 63–66.

Meru National Park
Some 60 miles NE of Mount Kenya, 1,000 to 3,400 ft up, 870 sq km (336 sq miles). Noted for Grevy's zebra and reticulated giraffe. See page 76.

Mount Kenya National Park
717 sq km (277 sq miles) round the upper slopes of snowtopped Mount Kenya, starting at 11,000 ft. Big game in the forests. Climbers' huts for mountaineers. See page 74.

Nairobi National Park
Unique in being only five miles from the city centre. 114 sq km (44 sq miles). Lions are the speciality. Open all year round. See page 53.

Lake Nakuru National Park
A bird sanctuary on Lake Nakuru, 100 miles from Nairobi in the Rift Valley. Thousands of flamingoes make the water seem pink from a distance. Altitude 5,765 ft. See page 59.

Samburu National Reserve
Near Isiolo in the north, 3,000 ft above sea level and therefore hot. Only 101 sq km (39 sq miles) of fairly dense bush but wildlife congregates at the river, where the main lodge is. See page 78.

Tsavo National Park
20,780 sq km (8,024 sq miles) of bush and occasional hills on the plains east of Kilimanjaro. Mostly 2,000–4,000 ft up. Divided into two sections, East and West, by the Nairobi-Mombasa road. Noted for great herds of elephant. See pages 89–92.

Game Conservation and Poachers
Finally, a word about poaching. The value of ivory and the Oriental belief that powdered rhino horn is an aphrodisiac, not to mention Western furriers' demands for leopard and other skins, coupled with a local desire for free meat, result in the game wardens fighting a constant battle to safeguard Kenya's wildlife from poaching by traps, poisoned arrows and other means. Indeed rhino are an endangered species. This is why hunting is banned as is the sale of ivory and game trophies. It is illegal to export any game product without a licence – which extends to sea shells and the elephant hair bracelets. The East African Wildlife Society (Box 20110 Nairobi) exists to help preserve wildlife and welcomes new members.

Transport and Safaris

Air
Kenya Airways runs scheduled services from Jomo Kenyatta Airport,

Nairobi, to Kisumu, Malindi and Mombasa. Fares are very reasonable by European standards. As mentioned in the General Information section, a number of charter firms operate from Wilson Airport, ten minutes drive from the city centre. Among them, Sunbird Aviation (Box 30103, telephone 501421) operates a daily scheduled service to airstrips in the Mara at Shs 1,100/- return. Pioneer Airlines (Box 42199, telephone 501509) operate regular services from Nairobi to Lamu. The Lamu return fare is Shs 2,300/-. The other principal charter firms are Africair (Box 45646, telephone 501210), Air Kenya (Box 30357, telephone 501601), CMC Aviation (Box 30135, telephone 501221) and Safari Air Services (Box 41951, telephone 501211). Of these, Africair has a particularly good reputation among businessmen and apart from the normal twin-engined aircraft, has a Learjet for charter. As already mentioned, flying can rival car hire for cost and is immensely quicker if you are going to distant parks and lodges. Depending on filling up available seats, costs run between Shs 2/60 and Shs 4/- per passenger mile. Whereas it used to be difficult to get through to Wilson Airport on the telephone, the service is now much improved.

Two charter companies operate at the coast: Sunbird Aviation operates at Mombasa (Box 84700, telephone 433320) and Malindi (Box 133, telephone 20069) and Cooper Skybird Air Charters at Mombasa (Box 99222, telephone 21443) and Malindi (Box 146, telephone 20860). In addition, Cooper Skybird operates a daily aircoach service from Mombasa to Lamu and from Malindi to Lamu.

Rail

Kenya Railways' main routes are from Nairobi to Mombasa, which goes overnight daily in both directions, and Nairobi to Kisumu, continuing on to Kampala in Uganda, which runs three times a week. Other trains serve Nyeri and Nanyuki. Trains going up-country are slow, because of the hills, but fares are low. The Nairobi to Mombasa service is in a class of its own – partly because there is still a vintage restaurant car, but mainly because it saves you a night in a hotel and is therefore highly competitive with even the cheap express buses. A first class single compartment, one way, costs Shs 432/- and a two-berth one Shs 324/- per person. Bedding, dinner and breakfast costs Shs 105/- per person.

Car Hire

Car hire is available in all main towns and from most hotels. Hertz-UTC (Box 42196 Nairobi, telephone 331960), Avis Rent a Car (Box 49795 Nairobi, telephone 336794) and Europcar (Box 49420 Nairobi, telephone 23013) are widely represented and you can leave their cars in Nairobi, Malindi or Mombasa at the end of the trip. However some local firms offer better value, notably Wheels Car Hire (Box 47173 Nairobi, telephone 336038) and Concorde Car Hire (Box 25053 Nairobi, telephone 747216). Although rates for small cars are broadly similar, there are wide variations when it comes to hiring a Range Rover or Toyota Land Cruiser. Typical self-drive charges for a Datsun 120 or other small cars is Shs 900/- a week, plus Shs 2/50 per km, plus collision damage insurance of Shs 50/- per day. A six-seat Land Rover would be from Shs 2,300/- to Shs 3,000/- per week plus Shs 5/- per km. Drivers must be over 23 years old and unless you have a major credit card

(American Express, Diners Club etc) you will have to put down a Shs 5,000/- deposit.

Buses
The Kenya Bus Company serves the whole country and very cheaply, but buses are liable to be very crowded. The Nairobi bus terminal is on Haile Selassie Avenue. A better alternative is the long distance taxis which ply between towns, and on which seats can be booked. The best known operation is called the Mombasa Peugeot Service (MPS), which operates to many other places. Its Nairobi booking office is on Duruma Road (telephone 334431). The fare to Mombasa or Nanyuki is around Shs 100/-. Ordinary taxis, however, are expensive.

Tour Operators and Travel Agents
Travel agents spring up in Kenya as fast as curio shops in Britain. It is important to distinguish between them and tour operators, who are separately licensed by the government, and who specialise in arranging safaris for overseas visitors. The reputable firms in each category have their own trade association.

Among the best tour operators, some of whom also have travel agency branches, are Abercrombie and Kent Ltd (Box 42196 Nairobi, telephone 334955), who have a London office (42 Sloane Street, London SW1, telephone 235 2992); United Touring Company (Head office Box 42196 Nairobi, telephone 331960); Across Africa Safaris (Box 49420 Nairobi, telephone 332744); Archers Tours (Box 40097 Nairobi, telephone 22871); African Tours and Hotels, a large concern managing hotels and lodges (Head office Box 30471 Nairobi, telephone 336976); Flamingo Tours (Box 44899 Nairobi, telephone 331360); Nilestar Tours (Box 42291 Nairobi, telephone 337392); Pan African Travel Organisation (Box 44209 Nairobi, telephone 333281); and Thorn Tree Safaris (Box 42475 Nairobi, telephone 25641).

Among the most reliable travel agents operating both in Nairobi and at the coast are Bunson Travel Service Ltd in Standard Street, Nairobi (Box 45456, telephone 21992), who also run A.A. Travel Ltd.

Many lodges and camps are represented in Nairobi by travel agents who accept their bookings and these are quoted where appropriate. But it has long been a feature of the Kenya safari scene that firms change their booking agents – and indeed often their names – more frequently than either a guide book or the telephone directory can keep up with. This is one good reason for making bookings through a well established agent or tour operator.

Safaris
Package tours now predominate in the safari business. Tours from half a day to 17 days are available locally, starting from either Nairobi or Mombasa. Many coast hotels arrange short flying safaris. Two of the most popular circuits are north to one of the tree hotels, Mount Kenya and Samburu possibly going on round to Lake Baringo and returning via Naivasha or the Mara; and south to the Amboseli and Tsavo National Parks. Any of the tour operators listed above will send details.

Nairobi is the centre for genuine field safaris tailored to individual clients' requirements. The main safari firms have already been mentioned in the section on Hunting and Photographic Safaris, on page 33. If you want to do your own thing completely, then it is possible to hire four-wheel drive vehicles and equipment from Safari Camp Services (Box 44801 Nairobi, telephone 891348). Habib's Cars Ltd on Haile Selassie Avenue, Nairobi (Box 48095, telephone 20463) also rent out small Suzuki four-wheel drive camping vehicles with full equipment at competitive rates. Tents and other camp gear can be hired from Bonar and Law Ltd (Box 42759, telephone 557355).

Various companies offer cheap camping expeditions, principally to Lake Turkana and to the Masai Mara. These offer excellent value if you are prepared to rough it: for example travelling in the back of a truck with seating but little protection from dust. The Turkana Bus is the best known, which does a seven-day trip to the famous lake. It leaves every second Saturday and costs Shs 2,200/- per person. Similarly the Wildlife Bus goes for seven days to Lake Nakuru and the Masai Mara. Both can be booked through Let's Go Travel, Standard Street, Nairobi (Box 60342, telephone 29540).

Nairobi

Nairobi lies 139 km (87 miles) south of the Equator and 480 km (300 miles) west of the Indian Ocean; and it is a surprising city, especially to anyone whose ideas of Africa revolve around tropical jungle. Its semi-skyscrapers soar white and dazzling as a mirage out of the surrounding Athi plains. Its avenues are adorned with statues and lined with great stretches of riotously-coloured bougainvillaea. The outer suburbs, occasionally visited by the lions who lived here before, are alive with hibiscus, oleanders and glorious blue-flowering jacaranda trees.

Although a few apartment blocks are being built in central Nairobi, the vast majority of the residents live well outside, normally going home for lunch and so creating four rush hours a day. The city limits include the prestigious suburb of Muthaiga, where government ministers and diplomats congregate in some extraordinary copies of English Tudor mansions and Spanish villas. There is even a replica of the Grand Trianon at Versailles, now the home of the Belgian Ambassador. Other favoured areas are Langata, 13 km (8 miles) out near the Nairobi National Park, and Karen, which has a pleasant country club. The land closer in is rapidly being built over, both with English sounding areas like Lavington and new African named housing estates, while elsewhere sprawling shanty towns have sprung up which the visitor is unlikely to see. The city is growing at a phenomenal rate. The population today is one million and is expected to be three million by the year 2000.

However the city centre remains small and despite all the new building, you can still trace all the stages of its hustling growth since it was a railway construction camp and pioneers' town. In 1902 the famous wildlife authority, Colonel Meinertzhagen, recorded in his diary – 'The only shop is a small tin hut which sells everything . . . The only hotel here is a wood and tin shanty. It stands in the only "street".' Today the main streets are still wide enough to turn a wagon and team of oxen. You can still find a few small shops – locally known as *dukas* – which have corrugated iron roofs behind one storey façades. But many hotels are now well up to international standards and there is a bloom of exciting modern architecture, like some of the government buildings, the extensions to the City Hall, the fine new buildings of the university and the Kenyatta Conference Centre tower.

The pleasant climate has had a lot to do with Nairobi's booming success. Being 5,500 ft up the nights are cool, while during the day the sun is warm, but the humidity is low. The temperature rarely exceeds 27°C (80°F).

Shopping
The main shopping streets are Kenyatta Avenue, intersecting Kimathi Street by the New Stanley Hotel, Moi Avenue (formerly Government Road), Standard Street, Kaunda Street, Mama Ngina Street and Tom Mboya Street. Within the central area, in walking distance of the New Stanley, you will find a wide variety of shops and the invariably helpful Information Bureau (telephone 23285), which is close to the Hilton.

Within this small central area of the city there are all the chemists, photographic shops, outfitters and general stores – such as Woolworths diagonally opposite the New Stanley Hotel – which the European visitor expects. The other facet of shopping is for local goods and souvenirs, which vary widely in price and quality. Curios are available in countless places, from sidewalk stalls to expensive studios. The main items are carved wooden animals and figurines, often only crudely made, baskets, daggers and spears, and beadwork. A good place to look is at the City Market, between Muindi Mbingu Street and Koinange Street. The main building is devoted to fruit and vegetables, while curios are sold in the open air behind. Always bargain. Prices are what you make them. Incidentally, this yellow painted structure may strike you as being a curious shape. It is. It was originally designed as an airship hangar in the 1930s but the R101 disaster put paid to the vision of airship services from Britain to Africa. The streets adjoining the City Market, such as Biashara Street, have many Asian shops selling everything from silk saris and silverwork to cheap suitcases, as well as African printed cloth lengths, called Kitenge, Khanga and Kikoi. The two former make up well into dresses. If you want to find a cheaper market, go to the hurly burly of the colourful Kariokor Market, a short taxi ride from the downtown area. Or try River Road – but guard your handbag or wallet.

Something different from mass produced curios are genuine tribal crafts. Two places to find them are African Heritage in Kenyatta Avenue and Studio Arts in Standard Street. The most celebrated East African carvings come from the Makonde people of southern Tanzania. These, like first edition books on Africana, are likely to be expensive, if they are old. Gallery Watatu in Standard Street stocks paintings, sculpture, prints and batiks, as does the African Cultural Gallery in Mama Ngina Street, while the East African Wildlife Society in the Hilton Hotel arcade has prints, drawings, beadwork and books, and Kumbu Kumbu, also in the Hilton, has sculptures.

A quite different local speciality is semi-precious stones and jewellery. As well as rubies, you will find tsavorite (a type of green garnet mined near the Tsavo National Park), tanzanite (a sapphire-like blue stone from Tanzania), aquamarines, tourmalines, opals, amethysts and jade. These are sold both as cut stones and mounted. Amber beads from Somalia can be a good buy as well, but make sure they do not have seams – if they do then they are

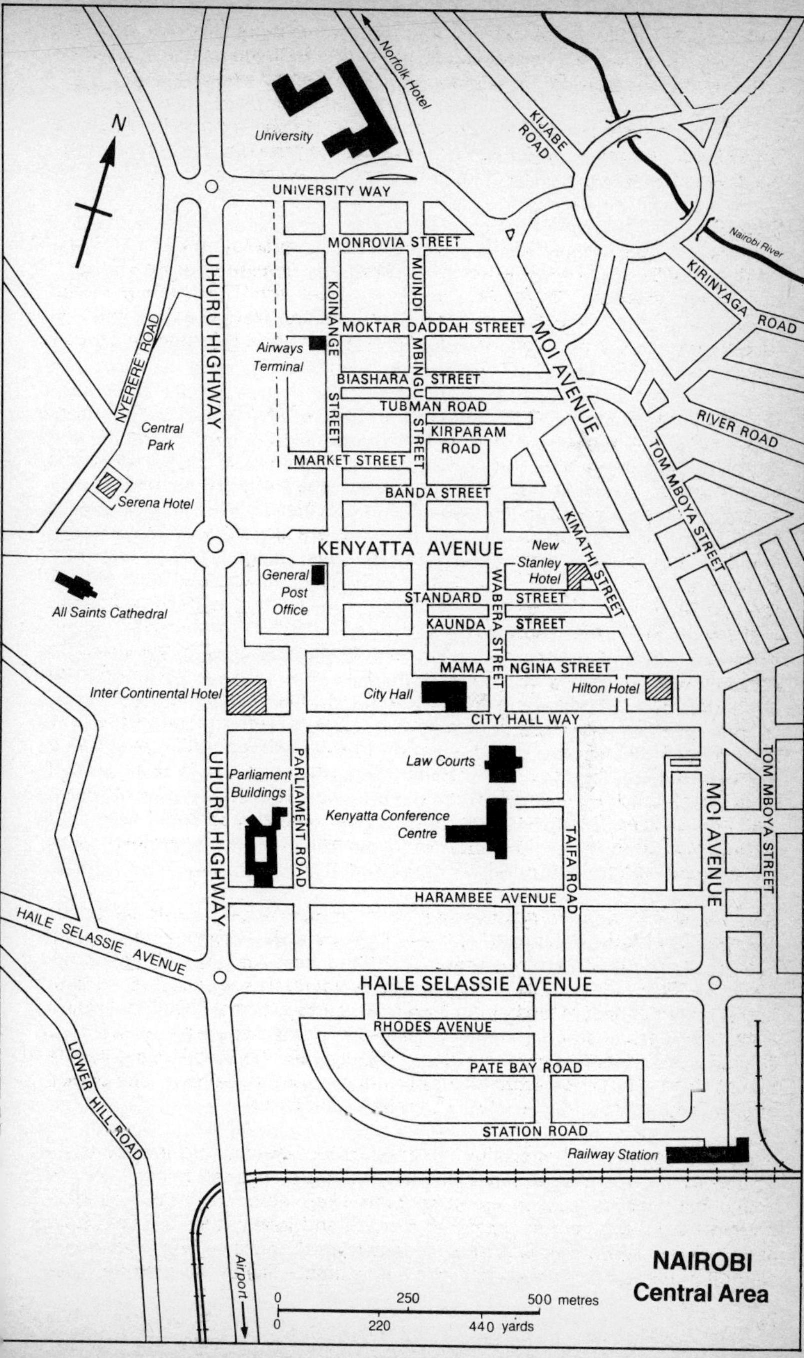

NAIROBI Central Area

plastic. Two reliable jewellery shops are Treasures and Crafts in Kaunda Street and Al-Safa Jewellers in the New Stanley Hotel. It is also worth visiting Rowland Ward Ltd, close to the New Stanley Hotel, to see the glass goblets which they engrave with wildlife scenes.

For safari clothing, either made to measure or off the peg, go to Colpro Ltd in Kimathi Street.

Schoutens, in the New Stanley arcade, are a good ladies' and men's hairdressers. Another men's barber is in the Six Eighty Hotel, while there are ladies' salons at the Norfolk, Hilton, Intercontinental and Serena hotels.

Tour operators and travel agents have already been covered within the Transport and Safaris section, as has Car Hire. Local tours from the city are dealt with below. Many international airlines have offices in the city centre. The American Express office is in the Express Travel Bureau in Standard Street. The best firm specialising in cheap (and legal) air travel is Air Systems Ltd in Moi Avenue (telephone 20171). The principal taxi company is called Kenatco (telephone 21561). It is not normal to hail taxis on the street, but there are taxi ranks at the main hotels and at the top of Kenyatta Avenue. Taxis are licensed by the City Council, but you should always agree the fare in advance, irrespective of the meter. A taxi to the Jomo Kenyatta International Airport would cost about Shs 160/- and to Wilson Airport about Shs 50/-.

Hotels

There are very few hotels in the city centre and they include the five Class A ones below, while almost all the cheaper ones are in the suburbs. (See page 41 for an explanation of class grading.) The most famous, and the oldest established, is the Norfolk (Box 40064, telephone 335422), once a pioneer's hotel. The Norfolk opened on Christmas Day 1904 and is part of Kenya's history, though it has been almost completely rebuilt since, and still has a countrified atmosphere, with old up-country wagons on the courtyard lawns. The Ibis Grill Room and the Lord Delamere Dining Room both serve à la carte meals. The terrace outside is a pleasant place for snacks or a drink. The Norfolk is situated opposite the university, about a kilometre from the city centre. It has a swimming pool.

The equally famous New Stanley (Box 30680, telephone 333233) has shops, an excellent restaurant which serves Scandinavian smörgåsbord on Fridays, and the open air Thorn Tree Cafe, which is a famous social rendez-vous, as is the first floor bar. The Hilton International Hotel (Box 30624, telephone 334000), also very central, was refurbished in 1982, has a good grill room in the Amboseli Restaurant upstairs, but like the Intercontinental Nairobi (Box 30667, telephone 335550), with its Le Chateau Restaurant, has more of an international character than an African one. Both have pools. Finally the Nairobi Serena (Box 46302, telephone 337978), set overlooking the Central Park on Kenyatta Avenue, has admirably large and well furnished rooms and a pool, but undistinguished food. Although 500 metres from the centre, it is inadvisable to walk to the Serena after dark.

The large PanAfric (Class B, Box 30486, telephone 720822), also at the far end of the Kenyatta Avenue extension, has a pool and a pleasant restaurant.

The Ambassadeur Hotel (Class C, Box 30680, telephone 333233) is well placed on Moi Avenue and has one of the best Indian restaurants in town, the Safeer. The Six Eighty Hotel (Class B, Box 43436, telephone 332680) is large and centrally located, with a Japanese restaurant, but is very much a businessman's hotel. Probably the best value for money within safe walking distance of the centre is the smaller Boulevard Hotel (Class C, Box 42831, telephone 27567) on Harry Thuku Road just beyond the Norfolk Hotel. It has an agreeable outlook and a swimming pool.

Among the smaller hotels with moderate prices one of the very best is the Fair View (Class D, Box 40842, telephone 723210) in Bishops Road, about one and a half km (one mile) from the centre and set in its own attractive gardens. About half the rooms have a bath or shower. Three Class C hotels that can be recommended and which all have swimming pools are the Jacaranda (Box 14287, telephone 742272) one and a half km (one mile) from the centre, out in Westlands; the Milimani (Box 30715, telephone 720760) a similar distance off in Milimani Road and the Safari Park (Box 45038, telephone Ruaraka 2311) 11 km (seven miles) off on the Thika Road which has a pool, tennis and a disco. Out there too is the Utalii Hotel (Class B, Box 30167, telephone Ruaraka 2540) which is the government's hotel staff training centre, with restaurant, pool and tennis courts.

Eating Out

At lunchtime you can have a snack meal at the Thorn Tree Cafe in the New Stanley, at the poolside restaurants in the other hotels, or upstairs in Jax Fashion Store on Kimathi Street. Marino's Restaurant in International House on Mama Ngina Street has an open air terrace and is good value for lunch, as is the Red Bull Paddock in the ICEA building on Kenyatta Avenue. In the evening it's amusing to go to the revolving restaurant on top of the Kenyatta Conference Centre and eat with a panoramic view of the city. The original Red Bull in Mama Ngina street is reliably good. Two first class French restaurants are Alan Bobbe's Bistro on Koinange Street and the French Cultural Centre's restaurant, also off Koinange Street. In the evening you must book at either. In Koinange Street, too, is the Hong Kong Restaurant, with good Chinese food but uninspiring decor. The Pagoda Restaurant by the Kenya cinema on Moi Avenue also serves appealing Chinese food. For sophisticated Indian dishes there is the excellent Minar Restaurant on Banda Street and the Safeer in the Ambassadeur Hotel, while you can get a reasonable curry at the Three Bells Restaurant on Tom Mboya Street. All the large hotels maintain good standards, though the Ibis Grill at the Norfolk is preeminent. Visitors can also enjoy temporary membership at the Bacchus Club in Standard Street, which is both a restaurant and a nightclub. Out of town, 15 minutes drive up the Langata Road, is the Carnivore, which specialises in every kind of meat from beef to venison, and has a garden bar. For a first class meal, you should expect to spend at least Shs 200/- without drinks.

An alternative is to try one of the many local establishments serving African food (see Food in the General Information section). This will be very cheap and quite an experience. The best guide is Kathy Eldon's detailed, informative and readable book *Eating Out* on sale at all bookshops. Or ask your hotel for advice. But do not expect glamourous surroundings, except in the African Heritage on Banda Street, which serves Ethiopian food in the evenings at normal city prices.

Entertainment and Nightlife

Nairobi has two casinos offering blackjack, chemin de fer, craps, roulette and other gambling, as well as evening floorshows and dancing. The International Casino is near the Museum and the Casino de Paradise is at the Safari Park hotel, 11 km (seven miles) out along the Thika Road.

The best conventional nightclub, as it were the Annabel's of Kenya, is the Bacchus Club in Standard Street, behind the New Stanley. The menu is extensive and excellent. Visitors can obtain an introduction from their hotels, but only Monday to Thursday. There is an entrance fee. Of the cheaper and more raucous local African nightclubs, which are an experience to visit, the best are the New Florida in Koinange Street and the Starlight in Milimani Road, near the PanAfric Hotel. Others are listed in *What's On In Kenya*, a free weekly magazine. There is a good disco at the Carnivore Restaurant on Saturday nights.

Entertainments of all kinds, including cinema and theatre programmes, are listed in *What's On In Kenya* and also in the Saturday edition of the *Daily Nation* newspaper. *Tourist's Kenya* is a free fortnightly.

There are 15 cinemas, showing new American, English and Indian films. The Donovan Maule Theatre Club is a delightfully designed small theatre with a resident company playing modern European and American dramas in repertory. Day membership, meals and drinks are available. The National Theatre has productions and concerts at irregular intervals, while the French Cultural Centre organises special film shows, concerts and talks. The World Wildlife Fund has regular showings of wildlife films there; details are posted in the lobbies of leading hotels.

Other Attractions

The National Museum is well worth a visit for its exhibits of wildlife and tribal ornaments. It has one of the largest collections of African butterflies in the world and over 1,000 species of birds. Also of special interest is the display dealing with prehistoric man in Kenya. The museum carries out a great deal of research and is particularly known for its discoveries on early man begun by the late Dr Louis Leakey, of world fame, whose son, Richard Leakey has carried on his work and is now the Museum's Director. Next door to the museum is an aviary and the Snake Park, which houses many species of snakes, with a fine collection of cobras, pythons and other rare varieties. There is also a crocodile pool and a tortoise pit. Incidentally, unless you actually tread on a snake, or corner it, you are most unlikely to be bitten. Snakes try to avoid meeting humans.

Among many other facilities, the city has a public library called the McMillan Memorial Library on Banda Street, an aquarium with over 300 species of fish on Mama Ngina Street and a magnificent arboretum some two km from the city centre near State House. It covers 80 acres and has many beautiful trees, both native and exotic. City Park, two miles from town on the Limuru Road, has extensive gardens and includes some of the indigenous forest, long since cut down elsewhere in the vicinity. If you're observant, you might see a troupe of vervet monkeys feeding and grooming themselves.

Places of Worship

The Roman Catholic cathedral, completed in 1963, is of strikingly modern design. It is built on the site of an earlier church which was the first stone building in Nairobi, and three of the bells from the old church now hang in the 200-foot campanile. The Protestant cathedral in Kenyatta Avenue is an older stone building set in an attractive garden. The Jamia mosque off Banda Street, has an arresting silver dome. There is a Jewish synagogue on University Way.

Sport

Racing and polo have long been favourite Kenyan sports. There are regular meetings at Nairobi racecourse, in a perfect setting, close to the city. Hurdle and flat races are also run at the Limuru Country Club 27 km (17 miles) out. This club has a first-rate 18-hole golf course too, and offers temporary membership to visitors, as do the Sigona Golf Club, the Muthaiga Golf Club (separate from Muthaiga Country Club), and the Royal Nairobi Golf Club. The Polo Club, where visitors are welcome, meets at Jamhuri Park on Wednesdays, Saturdays and Sundays, near where the Agricultural Society holds a tremendous five-day show every September. Parklands Sports Club (Box 40116, telephone 745164) welcomes temporary members to its swimming pool, tennis and squash courts. Finally, there is the toughest motor rally in the world, the three-day Kenya Safari, held every Easter. The city goes crazy over the Safari, the streets are hung with flags and all else is forgotten.

Nairobi National Park

For the live entertainment that most people come to see, the 115 sq km (40 sq mile) Nairobi National Park ranks first, and is so close to the city one could call it a suburb inhabited by animals. The main gate is on the Langata Road, some 10 km (six miles) from the city. At this gate are the Wildlife and Conservation Dept's offices, a well laid out Wildlife Education Centre and an animal orphanage sponsored by the World Wildlife Fund, which takes in abandoned and sick animals from all over Kenya, rearing them and later releasing those which are able to fend for themselves. The orphanage allows children to watch and participate in the feeding times.

Elongated in shape, and some 22 km long (14 miles), the Park's north eastern boundary is close to the Mombasa Road and it adjoins the Athi Plains, from which game come into it through the Kitengela corridor, the numbers building up at the end of the dry season in August. It contains a surprising variety of landscape and one continually flowing river, the Mbagathi. Entering through the main gate, you find yourself on a tarmac road alongside thickly wooded, hilly terrain. One possibility is to drive up – using the park map available at the gate – to Impala Point, where there is an observation hut with a panoramic view of the plains below. From here, preferably with the aid of binoculars, you will be able to see where herds of kongoni, zebra and wildebeest are grazing. You are quite likely to meet buffalo and occasional cheetah up in the wooded area behind this observation post, while on the plains there are lion, more often than not lying up in the shade of a thorn tree, or among some rocks. The early evening is the time to see them, when they are waking up from their afternoon siesta. Other wildlife include gazelle, giraffe, impala, baboons, crocodile and hippos in the river pools, leopard, cheetah, hyena, eland, warthog and ostrich. Remember not to get out of your car except at the signposted picnic places, and that this is still at your own risk. The Park is open all the year.

It is surprisingly easy to drive much further than you think you have done and have problems getting back to the main gate before it closes at 19.00. Don't forget there are other gates out on to the Mombasa Road, out to Langata among the woods and out to the Masai Lodge, which is a convenient place to cool off with a drink after game viewing, though at the time of writing the lodge was closed. The road is bad.

Ngong Hills

The hills that rise west of Nairobi National Park, forming a silhouette like the knuckles of a clenched fist, are the Ngongs, which rise to 8,000 ft. A visit to them makes an agreeable afternoon's excursion for a picnic and now features on many tour itineraries. On the way you pass through the Karen district, named after the Danish authoress Karen von Blixen, whose book *Out of Africa* about life on her farm here in the 1920s is a classic. Her farmhouse is now part of a government college on the Karen Road.

From Karen you continue to the township of Ngong, which is effectively where Masailand begins, and can quite easily find the dirt road up the hills if you turn right on reaching the township. This road, which is easily negotiable by ordinary cars in dry weather, leads to one of the peaks, near some radio masts. The view up here over the Rift Valley is magnificent, the air often being so clear that you can see a hundred miles or more and identify the great volcanoes in the Rift. You will sometimes see game here – zebra and giraffe especially – while buffalo lurk in the woods on the slopes. Two alternative, though longer, drives, are to turn left in Ngong and work your way along dirt roads at the foot of the Ngongs, passing among African farms, until you join the tarmac Magadi Road, which leads over the shoulder of the hills and provides magnificent views before it goes down into the Rift. Or you can turn left much sooner after leaving Nairobi, skirting the Nairobi National Park, and follow the Magadi Road the whole way. Magadi itself is dealt with in the next chapter.

The Great Rift Valley: Lakes Naivasha, Nakuru, Bogoria and Baringo

An excursion to see the Rift Valley, either from the Ngong Hills or via the old Naivasha Road, is one of the most popular tours from Nairobi. Yet the valley itself deserves a great deal more explanation than it sometimes gets. The Rift is one of the major features of the world's land-mass, a scar as clearly visible from 150,000 km out in space as the moon's continents are to us. Like the San Andreas fault in California, the Rift marks the boundary between two of the plates of which the earth's crust is composed. More than 20 million years ago, before the great mountain ranges of the Himalayas and the Andes had been created by the buckling of the surface, the land subsided along the fault lines which mark the boundaries of these two plates. The resultant valley, which is roughly 50 km (31 miles) wide and 2,000 ft deep in Kenya, stretches from Lake Baikal in Russia, down through the Red Sea, Ethiopia and Kenya to Tanzania and is dotted with lakes and volcanoes. A lesser rift valley associated with it runs down the present day borders of Uganda and Zaire, forming Lake Tanganyika – the second deepest lake in the world – and continuing through southern Tanzania into Mozambique.

Tremendous forces were needed to form this 3,200 km (2,000 miles) long valley and the subsidence left the crust of the earth thinner along its floor. In consequence hundreds of volcanoes erupted in the Rift, the largest of them being Kilimanjaro. Although so old, this volcanic activity is not extinct. The Shetani lava flow on the borders of Tsavo occurred only 200 years ago. Ol Donyo Lengai, the Masai 'Mountain of God' in Tanzania erupted in 1966, and the volcanoes south of Lake Turkana, where there are recent volcanic scarps, give forth jets of carbon dioxide from deep in the earth. The most powerful evidence of these releases is in Ethiopia, where the Danakil depression is vividly coloured by soda and salts and many of the string of Rift Valley lakes in Kenya and Tanzania are alkaline, both Magadi and Natron being covered in soda, or *trona* as it is called.

While the sections of the Rift which are most accessible are wild and impressive enough, others are still changing and the constant minor shifting in the surface has revealed important evidence about man's origin. Indeed the Rift in Kenya and Tanzania is virtually the territory of the Leakey family, since the famous palaeontologist, Dr Louis Leakey and his wife Mary, made their discoveries of the 1.8 million year old *Homo Habilis*, or handy man, at Olduvai (see Tanzania chapter) while their son, Richard Leakey, has unearthed even older fossil skeletons at Koobi Fora on the eastern shore of Lake Turkana (see Northern Kenya section).

From whichever way you approach the Rift, your first sight of it is likely to remain with you forever. Whether seen from the Ngong Hills, from the road to Magadi, from the old Naivasha Road – still the most dramatic view – or from the air as you fly to the Masai Mara, the Rift is one of the natural wonders of the world. Its floor is tawny red in times of drought, or dusty green after the rains. Its escarpment descends in a breathtaking series of terraces and its far off further wall rises dark purple against the blue sky, a procession of white clouds drifting across the volcanic peaks.

Olorgesaillie and Magadi

The road from Nairobi to Magadi is now tarmaced for its whole length of 110 km (68 miles). It branches left off the Langata Road not far beyond the main Nairobi National Park gate, skirts the Park fence and then passes through villages until it rises to cross the southern shoulder of the Ngong Hills at about 6,500 ft above sea level. From here, as already mentioned, there are panoramic views towards the lake, more than 4,500 ft below, with Tanzania and Lake Natron beyond and the Nguruman escarpment and the Loita Hills rising dramatically to the south west. It is a truly primeval landscape. You will notice many circular thorn-fenced *manyattas* (encampments) of the Masai, whose country this is for as far as the eye can see. (The Masai people are described in the chapter on Amboseli and Tsavo.) Their cattle share the valley floor with the game. Descending rapidly, the road takes you past Olorgesaillie, 64 km (40 miles) from Nairobi. Here Dr Louis Leakey excavated a prehistoric living site of the Pleistocene period, about 200,000 years old, originally discovered in 1893 by the man who gave the Great Rift Valley its name, the geologist, John Gregory. There is a field museum and a simple rest camp, where you have to bring your own food, bedding and crockery. Enquiries and bookings should be made to the Curator, the National Museum (Box 40658 Nairobi).

Lake Magadi, 1,900 ft, has a dirty white skin of *trona* on its surface, veined almost like marble, which is pumped out and converted commercially into soda ash and used for making glass. There is a small town, an airstrip and even a golf course. It is extremely hot, but the real attraction is the birdlife. Flamingoes, avocets and other waterbirds congregate around the lake, feeding off algae and apparently regarding the soda as a valuable protection from predators. This is a fact you can easily appreciate if you walk – or worse if you drive – too close. The lakeshore crust will collapse and leave you floundering, so binoculars or telephoto lenses are essential equipment for watching the birds. Further south Lake Natron is the greatest single breeding ground for flamingoes in East Africa because it offers similar protection.

The Nguruman escarpment, west of the lake, can be reached over very rough tracks. It is a magnificently unexplored area for foot safaris, varying from lowland plains to mountain forest, with fine views and an abundance of wildlife. However you need a fully self-contained camping expedition to tackle it.

Limuru, the Kedong Valley and Mayer's Ranch

The most scenically spectacular road to the Rift from Nairobi is not the recently constructed A104, but a turn off from it signed 'B3 Narok'. The A104 from Nairobi passes through Westlands, a major shopping centre, then climbs 2,000 feet up to Limuru, with the railway pursuing its more serpentine course close by. Limuru is delightfully wooded and green, having a much higher rainfall than Nairobi and indeed a totally different climate and landscape to the Langata side of the city. The Limuru Country Club has an excellent golf course and you can get a good meal at the Kentmere Club (telephone Kiambaa 253) on the Tigoni Road, which has residential accommodation and delightful gardens. Temporary membership is available to visitors.

Whereas the A104 road to Nakuru runs for some way along the top of the escarpment, giving occasional splendid panoramas of the Rift Valley, the old B3 road – which is liable to be potholed – reaches the Rift sooner. Suddenly you come out of a thin belt of forest, round a corner and there, 2,000 feet below you down an almost sheer escarpment, is the greatest valley in the world. Far ahead in its centre stands the clear cut cone of Mount Longonot, 9,111 ft high, hiding Lake Naivasha from sight. Euphorbia trees, candelabra-shaped succulents like giant cactuses, sprout on the steep slopes. Along the escarpment African boys sell a variety of souvenirs including attractive woven baskets and sheepskin hats, though unhappily there have been serious incidents and it is wiser not to stop. Approximately half way down a dirt road to the left leads to Mayer's Ranch, in the Kedong Valley, a favourite place for excursions, where you can watch traditional Masai dancing every afternoon in a *manyatta*, take as many photographs as you want without charge, and get tea. This ranch, along with the Bomas of Kenya in Langata, is the best place to see traditional dancing. The great white space-age aerial dish on the plains not far away transmits telephone calls by satellite to Europe and the United States, an extreme contrast to the life of the Masai, though it would be wrong to assume the Masai are backward. Many of their children now go to universities.

Continuing on the main road, at the bottom of the escarpment is a tiny chapel built by the Italian prisoners of war who made this road in 1942 to 1944. They had been captured during the campaign in Ethiopia. It is easy, driving along either here or on the new road above, to take for granted the engineering problems which the descent of the escarpment posed, especially for the railway, which has also had its alignment improved over the years. The problem of finding a safe gradient down from Limuru to the valley floor seriously held up construction of the line at the end of the last century. Both road and rail run through the Kedong valley towards the shoulder of Mount Longonot, before which is the turn off to Narok, the Loita Plains and the Masai Mara Game Reserve (see later chapter). The road is tarmaced as far as Narok.

Longonot can be climbed without undue difficulty: a dirt road leads from the Naivasha Road near Longonot Station, and there is a track up to and around the precipitous crater edge, from which you can look down the mile-wide crater, with eddies of steam rising among the trees on its floor. Needless to say, the view of the Rift is magnificent. The mountain's 52 sq km constitute a national reserve, but there is no security for vehicles parked at the designated viewing places. Further west, there are geysers and deep drilling is harnessing the natural steam jets to make electricity in geo-thermal plants, the residue of water being used for irrigation.

Naivasha

Irrigation for farming and tourism have brought about a considerable increase in activity around Lake Naivasha in the past decade. The township itself, only 97 km (60 miles) from Nairobi, is expanding rapidly, though it still has only ordinary *dukas* and the atmosphere of a frontier settlement, as so many up country places do. It used to be famous, not for its tourist facilities round the lake, which now make it a popular weekend retreat, but for the magnificent yellow-barked acacia thorn trees that grow in the neighbourhood – nicknamed 'fever trees' because it used to be believed the trees caused malaria. Actually, the trees grow along watercourses where mosquitoes can breed. The New Bell Inn (no classification) serves meals and snacks, while the newer Malaika Hotel (no classification) situated on a hill overlooking the town and the lake, offers full-board accommodation. Round the south side of Lake Naivasha (6,187 feet above sea level) is the Lake Naivasha Hotel (Class C, booking: Block Hotels, telephone Nairobi 22880) where all rooms have a private bathroom. There is a swimming pool, and punts and motorboats for fishing and bird watching can be hired, along with fishing tackle. The management offers a bottle of Scotch for the biggest fish caught each month. Six km (four miles) further along the South Lake Road is the less expensive Safariland Club (Box 72, telephone 29), which offers extensive facilities including riding and deserves an official lodge classification. It also has a camping site. Around the lake are a number of small marinas which offer facilities for boating, fishing, camping, water-skiing, including Fisherman's Camp near Hippo Point (Box 79, telephone Naivasha 5Y2) which has self-help accommodation.

From any of these places you can arrange a trip to Crescent Island, a bird and wildlife sanctuary where over 350 bird species have been recorded and Thomson's gazelle, waterbuck, monkeys and other wildlife live. A stroll with a pair of binoculars makes a very pleasant few hours. The lake shore is fringed by papyrus swamps inhabited by Goliath heron, storks, warblers, coot, purple gallinules and lily trotters, while cormorants, pelicans and others are often seen.

Crescent Island is in fact part of the rim of an ancient volcano and when the lake level is low the water it encloses forms a separate lake, with greater salinity than the main lake, which is one of the few freshwater lakes in the Rift. The reason remains mysterious. The water in the Sonachi Crater lake close by to the south west, for example, is highly saline. Farmers have taken advantage of the fresh water for extensive irrigation schemes. The Sulmac Flower Farm is the largest producer of carnations in the world, which like other flowers grown here are air-freighted to Europe. One of the lake's other features, and a less believable one when you see it on a calm day, is that even though its average depth is only 5 metres, storms blow up on it with great rapidity in the afternoons. Many people have drowned in its waters.

It has also suffered from a free-floating aquatic fern called *salvinia molesta*, which clogs the shores and from coypu, which have destroyed the lilies. Nonetheless it remains uniquely beautiful, set against a back-drop of mountains, which is why the late Joy Adamson, authoress of *Born Free*, made her home here, and it is hoped that the appallingly bad lake-shore road will be improved.

In the Pleistocene period, the lake was part of a vast area of water which included Lakes Elementeita and Nakuru, the outlet for which was the Njorowa Gorge, now generally known as Hell's Gate. This gorge, a mecca for rock climbers and ornithologists, shelters large herds of game and is due to be gazetted as a national park. It is reached by a turn-off through the Sulmac Ranch some five km (three miles) beyond the Lake Hotel. At the entrance is a lone rock pinnacle known as Fischer's Tower, which was once the plug of a volcano. The cliffs are the breeding ground of vultures, Verreaux's eagles, augur buzzard and thousands of swifts. The star attraction, if it can be found, is the lammergeyer, a bearded vulture rare in East Africa. Gazelle, and sometimes eland and buffalo, graze in the open valley beyond the gorge. If you penetrate far enough down here you will find natural steam jets and great clefts in the earth full of red volcanic rock, a reminder of the thinness of the earth's crust in the Rift. Hell's Gate indeed! The geo-thermal station is slightly further west and you can see its drilling masts.

East from Naivasha the road to the Kinangop Plateau leads on up to the Park Road across the Aberdare National Park to Nyeri (see page 71). The road reaches 10,000 ft above sea level and can be impassable in the rains. A board at the turn-off in Naivasha states whether this road is open.

At the small township of Gilgil a tarmac road branches off up the side of the valley to Nyahururu. Following the Nakuru Road you pass Lake Elementeita, a soda lake that is a nesting place for pelicans, greater flamingoes and sacred ibis. Though it is hard to imagine now, this route is close to the old caravan trail down which Arab traders took slaves and ivory from the interior to the coast and which the early European explorers followed inland, both suffering from attacks by the warlike Masai. Mythically, this was the road to *King Solomon's Mines* in Rider Haggard's famous novel. But it was the railway which opened the country up to European settlers and farming.

Prehistoric Sites
There are many remains of early man here. Gamble's Cave near Nakuru was occupied by Stone Age man from about 30,000 BC. There are other prehistoric sites at Hyrax Hill, just outside Nakuru, and at Kariandusi, near Gilgil. They are well signed and at Kariandusi there is a small site museum, with fossils of straight tusked elephant – a species which once ranged from Britain to South Africa – and an interesting display of hand axes and other primitive tools. These and the fossils were buried and preserved by movements of earth and volcanic ash during the later faulting phases of the Rift Valley. Next door to the site is a diatomite mine; the white product is used in making toothpaste, fertilisers and soaps.

Nakuru and Lake Nakuru National Park
Continuing along the new road (which as the signs tell you is part of a Trans-African Highway from Mombasa to Lagos) that now modernises a route which already carries a large volume of traffic to Uganda, the southern Sudan and eastern Zaire, you pass turn-offs to the Nakuru National Park.

Nakuru itself is the centre of a large farming area which holds an annual Agricultural Show in June. There are two hotels, the Stag's Head (unclassified, Box 143, telephone 42216), and the Midland (Class E, Box 908, telephone 41277). One good buy in the town is a locally made sheep-skin jacket, made to measure if you want. But the great attraction is the Lake Nakuru National Park, with its fantastic agglomeration of lesser flamingoes. At the end of the 1960s these were estimated to number between 1½ and 2 million and made the lake shore seem pink, while 389 species of other waterbirds have been recorded. In the mid-1970s the flamingoes appeared to desert the lake, possibly because the algae on which they feed had declined, and many went to Lake Bogoria further north. More recently they have returned. But in any case the 202 sq km Park is notable for other wildlife too, particularly pelicans, Defassa's waterbuck – there are some 3,000 here – Bohors reedbuck, found in the grasslands west of the lake, impala and Rothschild's giraffe, of which a small herd was introduced in 1977. The Park's road network has been improved and although many visitors come only on a day trip, there is ample accommodation. The Lake Nakuru Lodge (Class B, Box 561 Nakuru, bookings telephone Nairobi 20225) is built around a stone farmhouse on a hillside south east of the lake and is signed from the Gilgil to Nakuru road. Lion Hill Camp (Class B, bookings Box 48658 Nairobi, telephone 337916) offers full service under canvas. There are two campsites.

From Nakuru the main road leads on to Lake Victoria and to the upland towns of western Kenya, dealt with in a later chapter. You can also cross the 10,000 ft Mau summit to Narok and the Masai Mara, if the weather is dry. Or you can take advantage of the excellent new tarmac road to Lake Baringo and explore the Rift Valley further, including Lake Bogoria, only recently made easily accessible.

While at Nakuru you could visit the Menengai Crater, the second largest in the world and easily reached. Otherwise follow the signs out of the town to Baringo – if you are not stopping the turn is on the right between the conspicuously painted walls of State House and the town itself (when the Trans African highway reaches Nakuru the turn off will be outside the town). The road, the B4, passes through Kampi ya Moto and then crosses the Equator shortly beyond Mogotio. Disregard the sign to Bogoria here, unless you have four-wheel drive and plenty of time. The main road goes on through a changing landscape, which becomes drier and more reddish-brown in colour as you descend, with the thick green vegetation giving way to thorn scrub.

Lake Bogoria National Reserve

Lake Baringo first comes into sight in the far distance some 25 km (15 miles) before Marigat, lying dully in the valley centre. Then four km (two and a half miles) from the township at the top of a hill there is a crossroads with the Lake Bogoria National Reserve clearly signed to the right. A well graded dirt road leads down the 16 km (10 miles) past papyrus swamps to the Lobio entrance gate and office. The lake was formerly called Hannington after a missionary bishop who was murdered here.

The 107 sq km Reserve encompasses the whole of this soda lake, lying up against the eastern wall of the Rift, which here is thickly wooded and the haunt of both greater and lesser kudu. Leaving the entrance gate you drive down to the flat shore, the lake reflecting the sky in a way Lake Baringo's muddy waters do not, despite its being coloured green from the algae. It is a much more beautiful lake. Flocks of flamingoes are usually feeding close in and you can walk almost to the water.

At the lake side the road divides. The route around the east is rough, but the escarpment above is dramatic. The better road along the west leads to the hot springs, which belch sulphurous fumes. They are 13 km (8 miles) from Lobio though another central gate near them is planned. The road then continues to the south gate and on the 43 km (27 miles) to the main road, though it becomes rough. As well as birds and animals, the vegetation round Bogoria is interesting. The desert rose, a stumpy grey succulent bush with bright pink flowers, grows in many places. However, be warned that the lake is only 3,160 ft up and the area becomes very hot in the middle of the day. There are four campsites, the coolest being at Fig Tree. Enquire about them at the office at the Lobio gate. Opening hours of the Reserve are 07.00 to 18.00.

Kerio Valley and the Kalenjin People
Returning to the Baringo Road you descend to Marigat, a small dusty township near a river, where you will see a sign to Kabarnet. If you have the spare time for a major detour, it is well worth turning off west, up the escarpment to Kabarnet and on down to the outstandingly lovely Kerio Valley. Part of the valley, around the Kerio River Gorge, has been designated a national reserve. However the roads are rough. The climb up the Elgeyo escarpment to Tambach on the far side also provides magnificent views and takes you on to Eldoret and the farming land of the Uasin Gishu described in the next chapter. The Kabarnet Hotel (Class C, bookings Box 42013 Nairobi, telephone Kabarnet 35) is a convenient place to stop for a night.

The inhabitants of this area are the Kalenjin, whose combination of bravery and acclimatisation to high-altitude living has produced a number of world class athletes, including world record holder Henry Rono and the famous long distance runner Kipchoge Keino. The President of Kenya, the Hon Daniel arap Moi, is a member of the Tugen, a sub-tribe of the Kalenjin.

The Tugen live around Lake Baringo, which is the normal destination of travellers through Marigat. Continuing straight on, the lake is little more than 15 minutes drive, though the road here has several concrete drifts through river beds which could hold you up in the rainy seasons.

Lake Baringo
Reaching Baringo, the road terminates at a cluster of tin-roofed huts, rapidly growing to the size of a village. Before this there is a turn off to the Lake Baringo Club, very well run by Block Hotels (bookings Box 47557 Nairobi, telephone Nairobi 335807). The lodge has a swimming pool, looks over the lake and as well as organising boat trips, has a resident ornithologist who conducts bird-watching walks along the shore. A few hundred yards from the Club is the home of Mrs David Roberts, who has both a campsite with toilets and showers and self-catering rondavels available at Shs 45/- per night per person, bedding included (bookings Box 1051 Nakuru). The other lodge on the lake is the Island Camp, delightfully situated on the island in the centre and reached from a jetty roughly one and a half km (one mile) beyond the Club. A boat takes you across. The Island Camp (Class A, bookings through Thorn Tree Safaris, Box 42475 Nairobi, telephone 25941) has excellent food, a pool and 50 beds in double tents. Water skiing, boat trips, bird watching and visits to a Njemps fishing village or to Jonathan Leakey's snake farm can be arranged. Boats cost Shs 300/- an hour. Both the Island Camp and the Lake Baringo Club will meet visitors at the airstrip by the main road.

Although not a national park, Lake Baringo has great attractions. Hippo and crocodile are easily seen despite its muddy waters and the birdlife is astonishing: 448 species have been identified here, from goliath herons and fish eagles to tiny Madagascar bee-eaters and sparrow weavers, one mating pair of which may build as many as 15 nests in order to deceive snakes as to the nest they actually use. The lake is full of fish and although the Luo from Lake Victoria have moved in to capitalise on this asset, you can still see the local Njemps fishermen, sitting with knees bent on fragile rafts which they paddle far out into the lake. The Njemps are related to the Masai and their rafts are made from *ambatch* wood, which has similar properties to balsa, being extremely light and pliable. You can watch them being made if you visit a fishing village. The Tugen fish from more conventional boats, and are also pastoralists, though the land here is becoming sadly eroded from over grazing.

North from Baringo, the tarmac ceases but the dirt road round the north end of the lake and up to the Laikipia Plateau and Maralal is kept well graded. There is now a tourist circuit from Baringo right across to the Samburu National Reserve (and vice versa), which is a full seven hours dusty drive. If you are organising your own safari it is better to break the journey at Maralal, described in the Northern Kenya chapter, as is Lake Turkana.

The Masai Mara and Western Kenya

Although theoretically Western Kenya can be conveniently summarised as everything west of the Rift Valley, in practice road and rail communications towards Lake Victoria are forced northwards in a huge arc by the *massif* of the Mau Summit and its forests. Only a single road heads directly west to Narok and the magnificent game country of the Masai Mara and few visitors continue from there to the tea growing districts of Kericho and the shores of Lake Victoria. They normally either return to the capital or rejoin the Rift Valley route described in the previous chapter. Consequently we will deal first with the Masai Mara and then with the bulk of western Kenya.

The route to Narok and the Masai Mara

As mentioned earlier, the B3 road to Narok is signed off the A104 from Nairobi. Shortly after you reach the bottom of the Rift Valley escarpment you turn left again. From here on the surface is much better and you can reach Narok from Nairobi in two hours. On the way you pass the great volcano Suswa, which rears up on your left to 7,734 ft, and then climb steadily to cross the southern end of the Mau and enter one of the major wheat and barley growing areas of Kenya, where the Masai have turned to cash crop farming and the fields seem to stretch as wide as the Canadian prairies. Narok itself is both an important trading centre for the Masai and the last watering hole for tourists en route to the Mara. There are several petrol stations, *dukas* and two cafe/restaurants, neither of star quality, as well as a horde of souvenir sellers, principally offering traditional Masai beadwork, often at asking prices which can be higher than they are in Nairobi.

Beyond Narok the roads are murram, and often very bad. The first 18 km (11 miles) has been renewed and is reasonable, you then come to two junctions, where you need to keep your eyes open for lodge signs as conventional direction signs are very few. After crossing the Uaso Ngiro River (not to be confused with the Uaso Nyiro in the Samburu country) you come to a junction by some houses. The left turn here heads south to the Loita Hills, among which is the Masai settlement of Morijo, some 70 km (44 miles) from this turn-off. The Masai in these hills are among the most traditional and unchanged in Kenya. From Morijo a rough road swings round the western side of the hills to join the main Keekorok Road across the Loita Plains. Another rough road goes on to Entasekera (the Survey of Kenya map does not record this area accurately), from where a hunter's trail goes through to the spectacular Nguruman escarpment (see page 56). There are many colobus monkeys and leopard among the forests here. You must have four-wheel drive to negotiate the Loita Hills.

Returning to the road from Narok to the Mara, the second junction is a couple of km beyond the first. Signs for Keekorok Lodge, Cottar's Camp and others show that the left fork leads south west across the Loita Plains to Keekorok and the southern Mara. This is not a bad road and you should manage Narok to Keekorok in three to four hours. But the road straight ahead to the Mara River Bridge, Governor's Camp, Kichwa Tembo and the northern Mara is very poor. It can take five hours to the bridge. This is why many visitors use Caspair's daily scheduled air service from Nairobi. The road to the bridge starts off as the road to Sotik and western Kenya. For the Mara you branch left after the tiny settlement of Ngorengore. If you were going to Sotik and Kericho, you would find the road between Ngorengore and Kapkimolwa bad, but good thereafter. This point marks the boundary between the Masai and Kipsigis peoples.

Masai Mara Game Reserve

As can be seen from the map, the Masai Mara Game Reserve has only one natural boundary, which is the Esoit Oloololo escarpment to the west. This line of hills is an unmistakeable feature when you are there, cutting off the horizon behind Governor's Camp and the Mara River. The other boundaries of this 1,690 sq km (640 sq miles) reserve are arbitrary: The Tanzanian frontier to the south and an unmarked line across the Loita Plains to the north and east. The animals take no notice of any boundary except the escarpment and whether you are travelling to Keekorok or the Mara Bridge, you will see plenty of game as you cross the plains, though the greatest concentration is in the magnificent country of the Reserve because the waters of the Mara River play a vital part in the ecology of the area. In wildlife terms, the Mara is the extreme northern end of the Serengeti in Tanzania.

Every year in July and August a massive migration takes place from the southern Serengeti up to the Mara, where the river, draining off the Mau Summit, provides the water and pasture which by then has dried out further south. Literally millions of animals, principally wildebeest and zebra, move north in long columns along a route defined only by their inherited instincts, but which never changes. Within Kenya they cross first the Sand River, then the Talek and the Mara, always at the same points, charging through the waters in a tumbling cascade of bodies, uncaring how many drown. On the way up some of the cows will have calved and they guide their young across too. Otherwise they calve on the Loita Plains. For several months they graze here, and around December they re-group and return. As on the way up, the lions and other predators follow, preying on the stragglers and the calves. The migrations are one of the greatest wildlife spectacles anywhere and they depend to a great extent on the rains. It normally rains in December and the storms drive the herds south again.

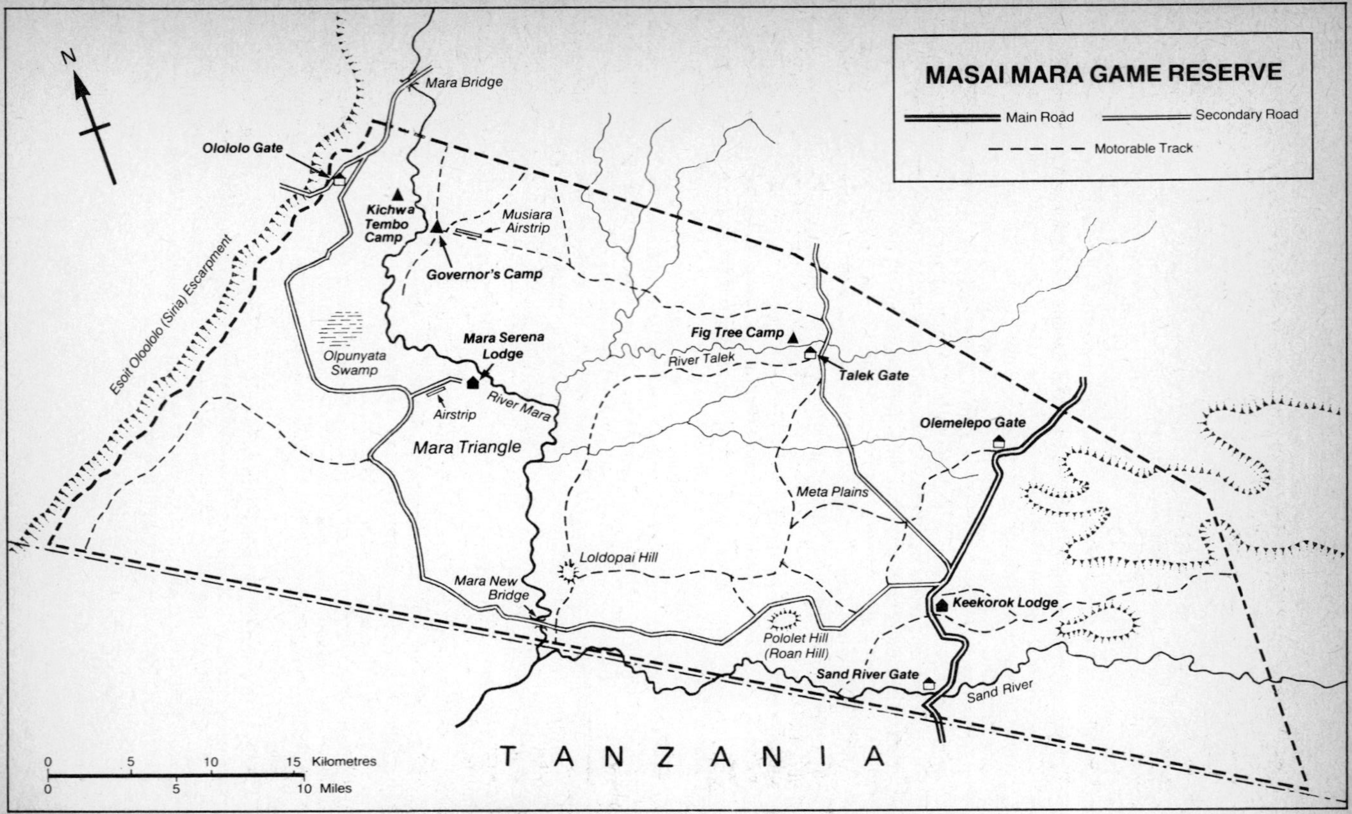

MASAI MARA GAME RESERVE
Main Road
Secondary Road
Motorable Track
N
Mara Bridge
Ololololo Gate
Kichwa Tembo Camp
Musiara Airstrip
Governor's Camp
Esoit Oloololo (Siria) Escarpment
Olpunyata Swamp
Mara Serena Lodge
Airstrip
River Mara
Mara Triangle
Fig Tree Camp
River Talek
Talek Gate
Olemelepo Gate
Meta Plains
Loldopai Hill
Mara New Bridge
Keekorok Lodge
Pololet Hill
(Roan Hill)
Sand River Gate
Sand River
TANZANIA
0 5 10 15 Kilometres
0 5 10 Miles

Above: Rare albino zebra on a game ranch below Mt Kenya. By Richard Cox
Below: Lion

Above left: Malachite kingfisher. By John Karmali
Above right: Young Fish Eagle. By Richard Cox
Below: Flamingos on Lake Nakuru. By Richard Cox

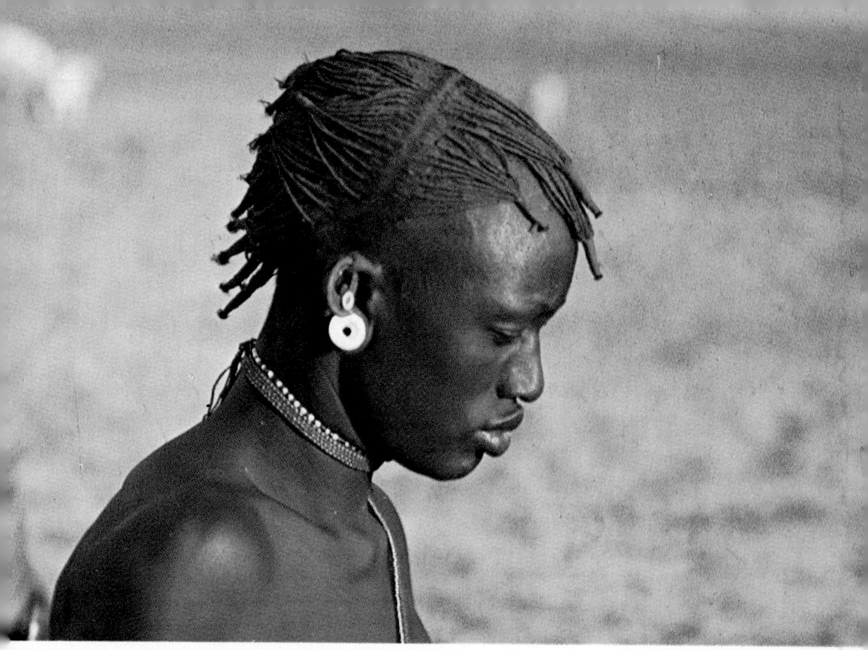

Above: Samburu moran of northern Kenya
Below: Herding goats and camels on the Tana River near Garissa. By Richard Cox

Above: Luo fishing boat on Lake Victoria. By Richard Cox
Below: Buffalo by a waterhole

This does not mean that there is no game in the Mara at other times. It includes a wide variety of country, from riverine forest to the open plains and supports a correspondingly wide range of game, from lion and the rest of the Big Five to hippo, crocodiles, roan antelope, topi – an antelope you will see standing on top of anthills to get a better view – countless gazelle, hyenas, silver backed jackals and many smaller animals. It has always been a splendid area for game viewing, but has only been opened up since the Tanzanian frontier was closed and Kenyan visitors could no longer go to the Serengeti.

There is only one good road around the Reserve and it goes from the Mara River Bridge round in the lee of the escarpment, past Kichwa Tembo Camp, across the Mara Triangle – a great game area between the river and the escarpment – then heads near one of the many hippo pools to the Mara New Bridge and on to Keekorok. There is also a road which traverses part of the Reserve on the way from Keekorok north to Narok via the Talek Gate. Otherwise all the routes are glorified game trails. There is a route directly across from the Musiara airstrip near Governor's Camp to Keekorok, which crosses drifts in several streams and rivers and is not at all easy to follow. In general, therefore, game runs tend to be done in the vicinity of the lodge or camp you are staying at.

Lodges and Camps

The oldest established lodge, though in design it is now completely modern, is Keekorok (Class A, bookings Box 47557 Nairobi, telephone 335807), situated in an area where hunters used to bring their clients to shoot lion. It has a pool and a tarmac airstrip. From here you can pursue the most unusual, if expensive, way to view game, namely from a hot air balloon. Balloon trips leave around 07.15, cover maybe 15 or 20 km of breathtaking cross country ride and finish with a champagne breakfast brought to wherever you have landed. Balloon trips can also be arranged from the newer Mara Serena Lodge (Class A, bookings Box 48690 Nairobi, telephone 338656), set on a hill in the Mara Triangle overlooking the river. Inspired architecturally by Masai huts, the lodge has a pool, its own airstrip and a hippo viewing platform by the river. You will notice rock hyraxes running around below the verandah in the evening. Unbelievably these furry creatures are not rodents, but are related by bone structure to the elephant.

There are no other lodges, but a number of excellent tented camps have been situated in good game viewing areas. The best known – and far and away the most expensive – is Governor's Camp (Class A, bookings Box 48217 Nairobi, telephone 331871). This is a site further north on the Mara River where colonial governors used to pitch camp in the old days, close to the Musiara airstrip and to very good game viewing. Governor's is usually heavily booked with German one-night tours from the coast and another, slightly less expensive camp, called Little Governor's (Class B) has been put up on the other side of the river, which has less of a package tour atmosphere. Governor's is strongly rivalled by Kichwa Tembo Camp (Class A, bookings Box 20224 Nairobi, telephone 335900). This has very comfortable tents, a semi-permanent dining room and bar and excellent food. It overlooks a wide area west of the river where a lot of game grazes.

Further on still, north of the Mara Bridge and some 30 minutes drive from the Reserve is the Mara River Camp (Class B, bookings Box 45456 Nairobi, telephone 21992). Reached by a turn-off from the Narok road about 2 km before the bridge, it has been improved lately. This was the base from which the artist Jonathan Scott worked on the drawings and photographs in the superb book *The Marsh Lions*, published by Collins, but there is not a lot of game in the immediate vicinity. Visits can be arranged to neighbouring Masai villages. On the opposite (western) bank of the river is the Italian-run Mara Sara Camp (not classified).

Finally, on the other side of the Reserve, are two quite different and worthwhile tented camps. Fig Tree Camp (Class A, Box 67868 Nairobi, telephone 21439) is well situated overlooking the Talek River, just outside the Reserve. It is reached most easily via Keekorok. Also outside the Reserve 17 km (10 miles from the Olmelepo gate) among hills to the east of the Keekorok Road, is Cottar's Camp (Class A, bookings Box 44191 Nairobi, telephone 27930). Here accommodation is partly in bandas (thatched bungalows) partly in tents, situated by a large stand of fig trees, and with its own airstrip. Run by a former hunter, Glen Cottar, it specialises in night drives and in game walks, neither of which can be done within the Reserve. There are elephants, buffalo, lion and leopard in the immediate area.

We have given these details of accommodation in the Mara because it is among the best of all areas in Kenya for people who want to make their own way, see a lot of game, and yet not be faced with the logistic problems attendant on safaris to remoter parts of the country.

From the Mara it is possible, with four-wheel drive, to ascend the escarpment where the country is quite different orchard bush and continue to Kisii and Lake Victoria, or take the Sotik Road already mentioned. However until these roads are improved most people will travel to western Kenya via Nakuru.

We have already described Nakuru. From the town – the fourth largest in Kenya – the railway and the A104 road continue north west to Eldoret and the Uasin Gishu Plateau and Uganda, while both road and rail branch off to Kisumu on Lake Victoria.

Eldoret

Eldoret itself is a farming centre and will be the home of Kenya's second university. It has a new hotel, the Sirikwa (Class B, Box 3361, telephone 31655) which is the obvious place to base oneself. There is very fine country to the east, especially the Kerio Valley (see page 61) while Kapsabet is to the south east, near the Kakamega Forest (described on page 68). The Kapsabet Hotel is classified E (Box 449, telephone 96). Near Kapsabet are the Nandi Hills, home of the warrior tribe and also of a mythical Nandi bear.

Efforts are being made to open up this area to visitors, and there is a Class D tourist hotel at Bungoma (Box 972, telephone 126) on the road to Tororo in Uganda. However there are more attractions further north beyond Kitale.

Kitale and Mount Elgon

Kitale, at the foot of Mount Elgon, is a pleasant township rather similar to Eldoret with one hotel, the Kitale (unclassified, Box 41, telephone 41) and is the stepping-off point for a visit to the Mount Elgon National Park 48 km (30 miles) away. This lies between 8,000 and 14,000 ft, being a strip of 65 square miles running up the side of the mountain, the 14,178 ft summit of which is in Uganda. The Park has herds of buffalo, elephant and eland, inhabiting the forests and moorland slopes, splendid bird life and caves filled with bats, into which you can venture if you have the nerve. Two of these caves, called Kitum and Makingeny, both within reach of the Park Road, have been largely gouged out over thousands of years by the small forest elephants: apparently to get at the sodium sulphate in the walls.

Mount Elgon can be climbed: for information contact the Mountain Club of Kenya or read Peter Robson's book *Mountains of Kenya*. You will pass through three main vegetation zones: montane rain forest, where you will see black and white colobus monkeys leaping among the tall trees; bamboo thickets; and finally alpine moorlands, where the same giant groundsels and lobelia grow as are found on Mount Kenya. This curious vegetation is described in the Mount Kenya chapter. You can reach the moorlands and return in a single day's strenuous climb. The nearest accommodation is at the Mount Elgon Lodge (Class C, bookings Box 30471 Nairobi, telephone 336858). The lodge is a converted farm house with beautiful views and is 25 km (15 miles) from Kitale.

The country north of Kitale is home to the Pokot tribe whose men wear conical ivory lip plugs and decorate their hair with ostrich feathers. While here you should stop 25 km (16 miles) north of Kitale at the Saiwa Swamp Park, a tiny tract of swampland created as a reserve for the sitatunga, a rare antelope with spiral horns and stripes on the flanks that stays up to its knees in water most of the time and feeds on swamp vegetation. The Park, which is only 1.9 sq km in area, has no entrance fee and no roads; you walk to the swamp and climb tree platforms for game viewing.

The dirt road past Saiwa goes to Kapenguria, principally famous for the trial of the late Mzee Jomo Kenyatta, Kenya's first President, ten years before Independence. A new road now runs from Kapenguria to skirt the Cherangani Hills into West Pokot and link with the older road to Lodwar and the west side of Lake Turkana (see later chapter). The Cheranganis themselves are some 80 km (50 miles) long, rise to 10,832 ft and offer lovely, if rugged, scenery and abundant birdlife, especially along the dramatic Kongelai escarpment.

Nakuru to Kisumu

The main Nakuru to Kisumu road passes a hotel at Molo, the Highlands (Class E, Box 142 Molo, telephone 50), just before the Eldoret turn-off. The hotel has its own golf course and tennis, riding and trout fishing are available. This is farming country, and Molo lamb is to Kenya what Canterbury lamb is to New Zealand.

Beyond Molo you toil up over the Mau Summit. In the Mau Forest live a few of the extremely shy Wanderobo tribe, diminutive honey-hunters, who dress in skins and are Kenya's oldest inhabitants.

Over on the other side of the summit is Ceylon in Africa, Kenya's great tea growing area, where the combination of morning sun and rain 335 days a year, together with the altitude, create ideal conditions. The fresh green bushes, close planted across the fields, are a fine sight and the product is among the world's best. Kericho is the centre of the tea cultivation and the Tea Hotel (Class C, Box 75, bookings telephone Nairobi 21855) is one of the better up-country hotels. Tennis, golf and trout fishing are available and visits to a tea estate can be arranged. Remember that you are 6,000 ft above sea level and that it is cool at night.

From Kericho the road brings you down to the Nyanza area and Kisumu, Kenya's port on Lake Victoria. The area round the Winam (formerly Kavirondo) Gulf here has seen a lot of mining. In the 1930s Kakamega, north of Kisumu, enjoyed a real old-style gold rush. Prospectors poured in from the USA, Canada and South Africa. It looked like another Yukon. Hotels and nightclubs sprang up. But the dream collapsed and the mines are flooded, though there is still some gold in them. However, the area's tourist potential has created a new hotel, the Kakamega Golf (Class C, bookings telephone Nairobi 332744). Fifteen km (9 miles) away is the only forest in Kenya that is West African in character. It was separated from the rest of the West African forest when the climate dried up, resulting in trees being replaced by grasslands. Kakamega Forest has many types of birds, butterflies, insects, trees and shrubs not found elsewhere in Kenya. There is an unfurnished do-it-yourself rest house which can be booked through The Forester (Box 88 Kakamega).

Kisumu

Kisumu is a busy commercial centre, Kenya's third largest town with several hotels, scheduled air services from Nairobi and a number of tourist attractions. As well as five E class hotels, there is the fully air-conditioned Sunset Hotel (Class C, Box 312, telephone 41100) which overlooks the lake, has a pool and pleasant barbecue lunches on Sundays. It is on the southern edge of town, near Hippo Point, appropriately named. Further on is the village of Dunga, where every morning scores of fishing boats set out at dawn to fish in the lake. Canoe races are traditional events. The Luo people of this area are both fishermen and farmers and you will find lake fish served all over the country. Among sporting facilities locally are golf, tennis and sailing. Kisumu used to be the starting point for steamer services around Lake Victoria and maybe one day they will be resumed. In the meantime you can take a four-hour trip on the M.V. Alestes to see Mount Homa and the Winam Gulf. The lake itself – the largest freshwater lake in the world and the size of Ireland – is one source of the Nile and equally a source of endless speculation amongst Victorian explorers, in the days before the railway reached Kisumu in December, 1901.

South of Kisumu, along the lake, there is a pelicanry at Oyugis, some 96 km (60 miles) from Kisumu, best visited between August and March. In the Homa Bay area there are many prehistoric remains, especially on Rusinga Island which can be reached by a ferry. Rusinga Island was the birthplace of the politician Tom Mboya and there is a memorial to him. The Homa Bay Hotel (Class E) is pleasantly situated overlooking the lake. 25 km (15 miles) beyond Homa Bay is the Lambwe Valley National Park, 308 sq km (46 sq miles), an area of grassland and bush where tsetse fly have prevented cattle raising in the past and so protected rare colonies of roan antelope and of Jackson's hartebeest.

Further inland the good Al road from Kisumu runs south to Kisii, a hill town which is the home base of Kenya's most renowned stone carvers. They work in the locally quarried soapstone, soft and almost rose coloured, making all sorts of objects from statuettes to tankards. A major statue by Elkana Ong'esa stands outside the Paris offices of UNESCO. The Al road leads to Tanzania and it is also possible to drive cross country to the Masai Mara.

North to Nyeri, the Aberdares, Mount Kenya and Meru

From Nairobi to Nyeri is all Kikuyuland, densely populated and so almost devoid of animal wildlife, though not of birds. The steep ridges that rise towards the Aberdares force the road to twist and climb even though the A2's re-routing to sweep east of Muranga avoids the worst, and the 155 km (96 miles), though all tarmac, is a two to two and a half hour drive, while the train puffs along for seven hours and five minutes.

Near Kiambu and Thika there are coffee, pineapple and sisal estates, easily visited by arrangement. Although better known for fine arabica coffee, Kenya is also the world's third largest producer of pineapples. Greater interest lies in the Kikuyu villages. The Kikuyu are Kenya's largest ethnic group (3.2 million in 1979) and originated as agriculturalists. A family may occupy three or more of the traditional round thatched huts, though increasingly they are being replaced by more modern rectangular houses. Both land and firewood are in short supply, which is why cattle graze on the road verges and you may see women pass by carrying loads of wood bought from traders, held up on their backs by a traditional leather thong passing round the forehead. Kikuyu women do much of the work on the family plots of land (*shambas* in Swahili), and some men have several wives. However, the Kikuyu are one of the most forward looking tribes in Africa and female emancipation has progressed rapidly since Independence: witness the number of African women holding responsible jobs in Nairobi.

The road by-passes Thika but it does pass the New Blue Posts Hotel, (Class E, Box 14 Thika, telephone 21303) a favourite stopping place since before Winston Churchill shot a lion nearby in 1908; it has recently been modernized. The hotel has an attractive garden overlooking the Chania Falls and a swimming pool. There is a lot of tall papyrus grass about like that from which the ancient Egyptians made paper. Elspeth Huxley wrote enchantingly about this neighbourhood in *The Flame Trees of Thika*. The town has developed industrially beyond recognition since, but the flame trees, which one sees in many other places too, still grow high and thick, with dark green foliage in which blossom dozens of reddish orange flowers, as vivid as shell-bursts.

Ol Doinyo Sapuk National Park

To the east of Thika rises a great humped hill, visible from far away. This is Ol Doinyo Sapuk, the name being Masai for 'The mountain of the buffalo', and there are buffalo, impala and bushbuck among its densely forested slopes as well as many birds, including the African harrier hawk. The mountain is a miniature national park of 18.4 sq km (7 sq miles). A road, negotiable by cars in dry weather, leads to the 7,041 ft summit. There is no admission charge. Just outside the Park boundary, close to the Thika Road, are the Fourteen Falls on the Mbagathi, spectacular particularly during the rains and a haunt of crocodiles. This river is better known as the Athi and flows all the way to the Indian Ocean, changing its name to the Galana in Tsavo East and to the Sabaki before it debouches north of Malindi.

Close to the Ol Doinyo Sapuk Park Road, in the bush, are the graves of two American pioneers, ennobled by the British. Before the Great War Sir Northrup and Lady McMillan owned Juja Farm near the mountain, where President Roosevelt stayed during his great safari, in an Edwardian wooden house shipped from India and re-assembled. Sir Northrup is commemorated by the McMillan Library in Nairobi.

The A2 also by-passes Muranga, formerly Fort Hall, where there is a church decorated with remarkable Goya-like mural paintings by a Chagga artist called Elimo Njau. They show the life and crucifixion of an African Christ in local landscape. Otherwise there is little more than Kikuyu villages and markets until you reach Nyeri, save that you may see the glaciered peak of Mount Kenya rising out of the clouds ahead of you. According to Kikuyu tradition it is the dwelling place of the god Ngai, and like Mount Olympus in Greece, it is shy of revealing itself, except in the early morning and the evening. Many of Kenya's Africans are animists, believing God resides in natural objects, like trees and hills. However about 25 percent are reckoned to be Christians.

Nyeri and Treetops
Nyeri, 5,750 ft up, is a well-laid-out township, with a 9-hole golf course and many excellent trout streams. It has an airfield but no scheduled airline services. The best tourist shop is in the Outspan Hotel (Class C, Box 24 Nyeri, bookings telephone Nairobi 22860) which is one of the best up-country hotels in East Africa, and stands one km from the centre of Nyeri in its own delightful grounds. It has extensive facilities including squash, tennis, trout fishing, swimming, car hire and riding. The hotel hires out all sporting equipment and fishing licences are cheap. Lord Baden Powell, founder of the Boy Scout movement, spent his last years at the Outspan – and very enjoyable they must have been. Nyeri's other Class C hotel is the Green Hills (Box 313 Nyeri, telephone 2017).

Trips to the world famous game-viewing hotel, Treetops, start with the excellent buffet lunch at the Outspan, after which a hunting car with a hunter escort takes you up into the forest, bringing you back next morning for breakfast. This is the only way of going to Treetops; you cannot simply drive there yourself, even if you could find the track. Book through Block Hotels (Box 47557 Nairobi, telephone 335807). The 1983 high season tariff was Shs 1,040/- per person including transfer from Nairobi but not including the Shs 30/- national park entrance fee.

Treetops stands by a pool on a low spur of the Aberdare Forest known as the Treetops salient. When it's raining in the bamboo higher up, which it often is because the rainfall is 80–100 inches a year, the game come down to drier ground in the salient and are attracted to Treetops itself by the adjacent salt licks and the pool. Buffalo, rhino, elephant, giant forest hog and antelope are common visitors. The Aberdare Park Warden says he has counted 500 elephant in the area at one time. They are kept off the farms below the forest by a ditch more than five miles long, six ft deep and six ft wide, the maintenance of which occupies at least 40 men all the year.

The original hotel was literally built in a tree in 1932, and the present Queen of England was staying there in 1952 when her father died and she acceded to the British throne. The visitor's book records that she and Prince Philip saw 50 elephants. The present hotel is larger, built 40 ft high on stilts among the trees and has a dining room, bar, bedrooms and verandahs, from which you get a grand circle view of the forest wildlife beneath, aided after dark by an artificial moon.

Aberdare National Park

The Park Road from Nyeri to the Aberdare National Park (the highest game park in the world) and Naivasha climbs 4,000 ft in 22 km (14 miles); it is closed in wet weather. It passes first through forest reserve, mainly planted with fast-growing exotic trees like gums; then into the alpine bamboo, feathery-leaved but impenetrably dense, with occasional bars of sunlight slanting down through it like rays from the windows of a great cathedral. Not far past the Park gate you suddenly emerge on to open moorland, 10,000 ft above sea level, and consisting of huge tussocks of grass. Up here you are allowed to leave your car and go up to 100 yds from the roads and rivers. There are two spectacular waterfalls on either side of a wide ravine. Karura dropping 894 ft in three stages, and Gura 791 ft, also in three stages. Especially near the water, there is fantastic growth of moss and giant vegetation, peculiar to the East African mountains. Groundsel and lobelias, small plants in Europe, reach 15 ft high here. It is as though one had suddenly been transported to Brobdingnag, the giants' country of *Gulliver's Travels.* In good weather the Park Road leads to superb views of the Rift as it descends on the other side of the Aberdares to the Kinangop Plateau and Naivasha. The road is partly tarmaced on the Naivasha side.

The wildlife in the Park is mostly shy, like the bongo. There are elephant, buffalo, rhino, eland, waterbuck, reedbuck, colobus monkey, serval cats, mountain buzzard, crowned hawk eagle and Jackson's francolin. The author saw a melanistic black leopard on one trip. There are a few lion and hyenas too. You may also come across patrols of game scouts, clad in green uniforms, and armed with rifles. Their job is checking on trespassers and poachers. Camping is not permitted.

Near the Park and the township of Mweiga is the Aberdare Country Club, a delightful former farmhouse, where riding and fishing are available. The Club is the starting-point for trips to The Ark, a 'tree hotel' rivalling Treetops for night game-viewing high in the forests of the Aberdares, where the animals you may see are similar, not forgetting the elusive bongo. The Ark is very well designed, with several terraces both open and glass enclosed. The King and Queen of Sweden are among notables who have stayed there. A visit starts with lunch at the Aberdare Country Club, followed by an 18 km (11 mile) drive up the forest road in the company of a professional hunter. You have dinner and spend the night at the lodge, returning after breakfast the following morning. The Club is classified C (bookings through Signet, Box 59749 Nairobi, telephone 335900). Charges for one night at the Ark, including transfer from Nairobi, were slightly less than for Treetops in 1983. The Club can also arrange day time game drives in the Aberdare salient.

Going north from Nyeri you can follow round the side of the Aberdares through Mweiga to Nyahururu (Thomson's Falls) and then strike north to Rumuruti on what is a much improved route to Maralal, being tarmac to Rumuruti and well graded murram to Saguta. The alternative is to go directly north to Naromoru, Nanyuki and Mount Kenya. We deal with the Rumuruti direction first.

Nyeri to Nyahururu and Rumuruti

The fast tarmac road from Nyeri to Nyahururu, a distance of 115 km (74 miles) takes you across the glorious plains of Laikipia which is ranching land dotted with umbrella thorns and spiritually akin to Texas. Here Santa Gertrudis is as much a household word as Hereford or Boran, these last being the African humped cattle with which imported stock are often crossed to combine yield with resistance to local conditions.

Cattle have a tough life out here, what with tropical fevers and ticks, which they catch all too easily from the buffalo, buck, giraffe and other game that also wander over Laikipia. However there is no tsetse fly, so many farmers keep horses. Among the largest ranches are one belonging to the Paris art dealer Wildenstein; the Ol Pegeta Ranch of the Saudi Arabian millionaire, Adnan Kashoggi, where game is preserved alongside 16,000 head of cattle; and the American-owned Solio Ranch, which doubles as a private game reserve. Solio can be visited by arrangement with the Aberdare Country Club for a Shs 100/- fee per person, plus vehicle charges. The ranch is beyond Mweiga on the Nyahururu Road and you are more certain to see rhino there than anywhere else in Kenya. Finally the Sangare Ranch of 25,000 acres has a small fully-serviced private lodge by a lake with riding and fishing. There is a lot of game. (Enquiries to Prettejohn, Box 24 Mweiga, telephone 20.) Driving on past here you will catch sight of the Aberdare peaks on your left, notably Satima (13,120 ft). The Ngobit River is a fine trout stream.

Nyahururu

Nyahururu, a township formerly called Thomson's Falls after the same explorer who gave the 'Tommy' gazelle its name, has a hotel, the Thomson's Falls Lodge, (Class E, Box 38, telephone 6) right by the waterfall and with gardens overlooking the dramatic gorge below it. The rooms are comfortable, if simple, and have private baths. Something to look out for here are locally-made carpets from the small Kufuma Factory (telephone Nyahururu 16). Woven in muted oatmeal-brown and grey colours, either in flat weave or pile, these are priced at from Shs 725/- for a small rug, upwards. They are obtainable in Nairobi through Jax Boutique in Kimathi Street.

From Nyahururu a branch railway line and a road run south to Gilgil (see page 59) via Ol Kalou, through the farming country known before World War II as the 'Happy Valley'. Here the more riotous of the British settlers lived, people whose extraordinary life style has been brought alive again by James Fox's book *White Mischief*, about the murder in 1940 of Lord Errol. A branch from this road goes to Nakuru and another minor road winds to Nakuru via the attractive farming country of Subukia, with its stone Norman-style church, in fact built in 1951. Using these roads you can complete a circuit of the Aberdares and return to Nairobi along the Rift Valley.

North from Nyahururu a much improved dirt road goes the 34 km (21 miles) across Laikipia to Rumuruti, where there is an airstrip, but no hotel. From here it continues the 80 km (50 miles) to Maralal, one of the gateways to Northern Kenya, described in the next chapter. On the way you pass the turn-off to one of a small number of private ranches which have been opened up to visitors, Colcheccio.

Colcheccio

The Colcheccio Club (not classified, Box 50 Rumuruti) is a ranch-style farmhouse situated on a bluff overlooking a valley with greater kudu and other game wandering below and Mount Kenya in the distance. On the ranch's 73,000 acres you can see large herds of plains game, including buffalo and Grevy's zebra. It has a pool, tennis court, riding and an airstrip, and a pleasantly relaxed atmosphere. Prices are high but include game drives. Accommodation is in cottages, each with its own bathroom. It is 30 km (19 miles) north of Rumuruti, near Kirimum. Make sure to obtain precise directions before setting out.

Nyeri to Mount Kenya and Meru

The tarmac road from Nyeri to Nanyuki, a distance of 51 km (32 miles) is good. Before Naromoru is the signpost to the Mountain Lodge (Bookings Box 30471 Nairobi, telephone 336858) the third of the 'tree hotels'. The fourth, The Secret Valley, was destroyed by fire. 7,200 ft up, it is one of the best high-altitude bird watching spots. It also attracts large numbers of big game. You must arrive between 16.00 and 18.30 hours. The 1983 price was Shs 920/- double for dinner, bed and breakfast. The lodge can also be reached from the Karatina-Nyeri road, if you are coming direct from Nairobi.

Naro Moru

The trading post of Naro Moru, once the centre of a European farming district, is now farmed by Africans. Lying on the lower slopes of Mount Kenya, it is attractive country and many of the scenes in *Born Free*, the film of Joy Adamson's book about her tame lions, were shot around here.

About half a mile from the main road is the comfortable Naro Moru River Lodge (Class C, Box 18 Naro Moru, telephone 23). Set on the river, which is stocked with rainbow and brown trout, the lodge has pleasant cedar log cabins, each with its own bathroom. Cheaper self-service chalets for two or more people are also available. As well as riding, walking, fishing and bird watching (Jackson's Francolin and Lanner Falcon are among local species), the lodge offers foot safaris up Mount Kenya by the Teleki route. These involve no rock climbing, though you need to be reasonably healthy. They last 2 to 4 days and cost from Shs 1,000/- to Shs 2,500/- per person. A one-day trip is also possible as is a full scale mountaineering ascent. Clothing and equipment can be hired.

Mount Kenya and the Aberdares also have several fishing camps for the ardent trout fisherman, including Thiba, Thego, Kimakia and Kiandongoro. At these places you must bring your own food, bedding and equipment, but there are hot and cold water, beds and cooking equipment. (Further information from the Fisheries Dept, Box 40241 Nairobi.) Some trips to Mountain Lodge include a luncheon stop at Thego Fishing Camp.

Nanyuki

Nanyuki, a railhead and shopping town with banks, chemists and a hospital, is mainly dedicated to farming and to the Kenya Air Force and Army. It is the real stepping-off point for Northern Kenya and a place to climb Mount Kenya from. It lies 6,400 ft up at the foot of the mountain and smack on the Equator. In fact the Silverbeck Hotel used to claim the Line ran across its bar floor, so that you could be in the northern hemisphere while your drinking companion was in the southern. Unhappily the bar was burnt down and awaits rebuilding. A couple of miles out is the renowned Mount Kenya Safari Club (Class A, bookings Box 54546 Nairobi). Calmly luxurious, it has its own golf, airstrip, bowls, swimming pool, sauna baths, riding, fishing, displays of traditional dancing – the lot in fact. Peacocks wander on the terrace and the 200 staff have looked after many of the world's famous people. Temporary membership is available. Adjoining the club is the Mount Kenya Game Ranch, founded by the late William Holden, the film star, who was part owner of the club. The Ranch provides a haven for animals whose habitat is threatened.

Nanyuki used to be a safari centre, and safaris still start from here. However one of the organisers, John Alexander, is now based in Nairobi (Box 20127, telephone 891477) as is David Allen (Box 40132, telephone 60365) and Julian McKeand is running his notable camel safaris from Lewa Downs (Private Bag, Isiolo).

Mount Kenya National Park

When the German missionary Ludwig Krapf sent home reports that he had observed a snow-capped mountain on the Equator, no-one in Europe believed him. Eminent authorities declared such a thing to be impossible. Today mountaineers come from all over the world to tackle the difficult ascent as a training ground for the Himalayas. In practice, how much of a challenge you make of climbing Mount Kenya depends largely on you. By merely walking to the top hut you are getting higher than Mont Blanc in the Alps, and the trek up through the forests of bamboo and podo and across the moorland is rewarding, though not for anyone who gets short of breath at normal altitudes. There are the same animals as on the Aberdares, plus some of the most lovely birds in Africa – malachite sunbirds, golden-winged sunbirds, yellow francolin and the Abyssinian long-eared owl, and the same curious 'old man's beard' hanging ghostlike from the trees. In four days you can 'conquer' the easiest peak, Lenana, 16,355 ft, and see the glaciers, the 32 lakes and tarns and the giant vegetation of the mountain slopes.

This vegetation is unique to the East African mountains. It includes blue-flowering lobelias which grow to 10 ft high and giant groundsel which reach 19 ft. They have apparently developed in response to the extremes of freezing cold at night and hot tropical sun by day, a variation made greater by the altitude. Their long stems are insulated by layers of dead leaves, helping protect them from the particularly cold air lying on the surface at night.

Walking to the moorland and the tarns is easy. However reaching the twin summits of Batian (17,058 ft) and Nelion (17,022 ft) is a different matter. There are very high winds, tricky rock, shifting ice and the risk of contracting fatal pulmonary oedema from prolonged effort at this altitude. The peaks have claimed many lives and the Austrian mountain rescue service has been training Kenyans for rescue work. Because the mountain is on the Equator, the south side is in sunshine during the first six months of the year and the north in the second, thus the time of year dictates which face you climb. The best seasons are the driest periods of mid-January to late February, late August and September. Batian and Nelion, joined by a ridge called the Gate of Mists, are actually hard cores of rock exposed by erosion of the crater rim, for Mount Kenya, like Kilimanjaro, is an extinct volcano. More information can be had from the safari firms, or the national parks or the Mountain Club of Kenya (Box 45741, Nairobi).

The Mountain Club publishes the excellent *Guide Book to Mount Kenya and Kilimanjaro* with full details of climbing routes and sections on the geology, flora and fauna of the mountain. There is accommodation in chalets at the Meteorological Station on the Naro Moru track, which can be booked either through the Naro Moru River Lodge or through the Park Warden (Box 69, Naro Moru). The Mountain Club's huts further up can also be booked through the River Lodge, but their facilities – anyway very basic – have been sadly abused by tourists who are not true climbers.

Of the various tracks up the mountain, the best known are the Naro Moru track which enters the Park through the main gate at 8,000 ft and continues to 10,000 ft and the Sirimon track from the north west which reaches 11,000 ft. The Carr track from the Meru side reaches 14,000 ft. Obviously, all demand four-wheel drive and dry weather. The Park itself starts around the 10,000 ft contour, enclosing only part of the forest in its 600 sq km (231 sq miles). You can get some idea of the huge scale of the mountain by comparing it to Britain. If its 56 km (35 miles) base was superimposed on the Home Counties, it would stretch from central London to Aldershot.

Towards Isiolo and Meru
From Nanyuki the main tarmac road climbs steadily north east through Timau, where a sign to the right indicates the Kentrout Trout Farm (telephone Timau 14) which has a restaurant and is a pleasant, shady spot to break a long journey. Here you are coming to another of Kenya's wheat growing areas, with huge fields which suddenly end as the road descends over the escarpment to the north revealing a truly magnificent panorama towards the Samburu country. The escarpment drops almost 5,000 ft in under 30 km (19 miles), described in the next chapter. A short way down the road divides, the A2 continuing to Isiolo, while the right hand fork leads around the contours of Mount Kenya to Meru, with the Meru Hills on the left.

If you continue some 2 km past this junction on the Isiolo Road you pass a sign on a rock indicating Wilderness Trails. This is the entrance to a private 40,000-acre ranch where the owner, David Craig, runs one of the best private tented camps in Kenya. Not unduly luxurious, it is set by a stream with semi-permanent dining room, excellent farm food and a great variety of facilities, from game drives and walks, to riding, visiting a pre-historic hand axe site and watching falconry. Game on the ranch runs from elephant down to bush babies and bat eared foxes, including the long necked gerenuk, leopard and cheetah. In 1983 the cost was Shs 1,500/- double per day including all facilities. The address is Private Bag, Isiolo (bookings through Bateleur Safaris, Box 42562 Nairobi, telephone Nairobi 27048, mornings only). The ranch is the base for Julian McKeand's camel safaris, which operate in the Samburu country further north and are described in the next chapter.

Embu and Meru
Both this road to the Meru and Embu country round the eastern side of Mount Kenya, and the direct road from Nairobi, which forks off the Nairobi to Nyeri road at Sagana, are tarmaced. The direct road from Nairobi to Embu is 131 km (82 miles) and there is an all-weather murram road from Embu to Meru, which although it may some day be tarmaced, remains one of the most tortuous stretches of the Safari Rally. At Embu there is a pleasant small hotel set in well kept gardens called the Izaak Walton Inn – named after the famous angler because of the fine trout fishing in the mountain streams here (Class E, Box 1 Embu, bookings telephone Nairobi 27828).

The Meru district is densely populated and mainly known for fishing, rare butterflies and Meru oak, one of Kenya's most beautiful indigenous woods. Plus, of course, the Meru National Park. There is a small museum in Meru town, with displays of traditional dress and ornaments.

Meru National Park
From Meru town to Meru National Park is 78 km (49 miles). The road, tarmaced as far as Maua, can be negotiated by any kind of vehicle. Meru National Park's 821 sq km (317 sq miles) contain an excellent system of roads and tracks, plus several airstrips. By the Meru National Park runs the Tana River, 704 km (440 miles) long, which winds through the Northern Frontier down to the Indian Ocean near Lamu. Up here its banks attract wildlife like jam does flies and a motorboat is available for river exploration. There is plenty of game in the reserve, including reticulated giraffe and Grevy's zebra, lion, leopard, black rhino, elephant, buck and a great variety of birds. A herd of white rhino, previously extinct in the area, was introduced here from South Africa; they are now breeding successfully and may be seen at their compound near Park headquarters or else feeding in the vicinity, escorted by a ranger. The altitude of the Park varies from about 1,000 ft along the Tana to 3,400 ft in the Nyambeni foothills. West of Leopard's Rock there is a wilderness area with no roads, while the site of Elsa's camp, used by the late Joy Adamson, is on the Ura River in the south of the Park.

There are several kinds of accommodation available in or adjacent to the Park. The Meru Mulika Lodge (Class B, bookings Box 30471 Nairobi, telephone 336858) has comfortable rooms in rondavels, a water hole where game comes to drink and a swimming pool. A few miles away is Leopard Rock Self-help Lodge, a self-service lodge with ten bandas (huts), each with private bathroom. The only thing you need take is your own food. Bookings can be made through AA Travel (Box 14982 Nairobi, telephone 720382). There is a public campsite near Park headquarters and also the Bwatherongi Bandas, (self-help), both of which can be booked through the Park Warden (Box 162, Meru).

Kora National Reserve
Adjacent to Meru National Park, on the south of the Tana River, is the Kora National Reserve, created largely through the effort of George Adamson; he still lives here, rehabilitating tame lions for release though he is now in his 80s. Kora is 1,787 sq km (about 500 sq miles) of remote, dry bush country with game similar to that found in Meru National Park. There are tracks negotiable by ordinary cars, but no accommodation as yet. Camping is permitted.

Northern Kenya: The Samburu, Maralal, Marsabit, Lake Turkana

The vast semi-desert that stretches north of the Highlands and the Tana River to the frontiers of the Sudan, Ethiopia and Somalia is more than half of Kenya. In colonial days it was known as the Northern Frontier District, or NFD, which had a mystique all of its own. Today it is split between the Rift Valley Province in the west and the Eastern and North Eastern Provinces (the latter being dealt with in the next chapter). But the 'jade sea' of Lake Turkana continues to be a magnet to the adventurous and it is impossible not to be moved by one's first sight of the north. There are three main routes. Via Baringo or Kitale through West Pokot to Lodwar, west of the lake. Via Maralal to the eastern shore. Or by the Great North Road via Nanyuki and Isiolo to Marsabit and Moyale. Approaching from Nanyuki on the main road through Timau to Isiolo you find yourself abruptly at the top of a sloping 4,000 ft escarpment. Spreading away below is a reddish landscape out of which occasional mountains rise, hot and barren, save for scrub – and fiercely exciting. In it, rivers mysteriously disappear, as the Uaso Nyiro does into the Lorian Swamp, or run for miles beneath the sand. Elephant are coated with red dust. The nomads herding their goats and camels and fat-tailed sheep to water holes remind one of Biblical scenes, though most of them are Moslems.

The nearer part of the north has become a tourist circuit of growing importance, taking in Nanyuki, the Samburu National Reserve, swinging round north west through Wamba to Maralal and returning to Nairobi via Lake Baringo. The roads on this circuit have been greatly improved. But further north they are difficult if not impassable in ordinary cars and the north remains inaccessible except to those who make special plans. Only well organised safaris survive. One firm which specialises in arranging them is Ker Downey Safaris (Box 41822 Nairobi, telephone 556466) who have taken Britain's Prince Charles there. Julian McKeand, as well as doing the short camel safaris described further on (page 80), undertakes longer ones as far as the lake if clients require it.

The start of the route north via Kitale has already been described (page 67). There are plans to tarmac the road as far as Lodwar, from which a road is being constructed to the southern Sudan, a major enterprise. From Lodwar you have access to both Ferguson's Gulf and Eliye Springs on Lake Turkana, where there are fishing lodges, described under Lake Turkana (page 81).

Maralal and the Samburu

The Maralal route, either from Lake Baringo or Rumuruti, has also been greatly improved. Totalling 348 km (217 miles) from Nairobi via Rumuruti, the last 112 km (70 miles) run across the Lorochi Plateau and the Karisia Hills, which used to be a favourite hunting area in the old days and still has a fair amount of game. Maralal itself is a centre for the Samburu and has the atmosphere of a frontier town, the dusty main street crowded with tribespeople, the market place loaded with bangles, necklaces and beadwork. Note that petrol supplies are erratic.

The Samburu are a tall, handsome people. The women adorn themselves with coil upon coil of heavy bead necklaces and the *moran* decorate themselves with red ochre and are every inch noblemen. They customarily wear loincloths of a vivid red and stand, spear in hand, on one leg, the other foot raised behind. The *moran* have to serve as warriors for at least ten years before they are allowed to marry. Like the Masai they are nomadic cattle owners and construct very similar *manyattas*, with low huts roofed with mud and dung. They inhabit a large tract, stretching east beyond the Isiolo to Marsabit Road and north to the Ndoto Hills and are associated with the Rendille beyond. The Maralal Safari Lodge (Class B, bookings Thorn Tree Safaris, Box 42475, telephone 25641) is very well situated within the area of the Maralal National Sanctuary. It has a waterhole which attracts game in the evening and a hide up on the hill where bait is put out for leopard. The lodge has comfortable cedar log cottages, reminiscent of Swiss chalets, each with its own bathroom.

About 24 km (15 miles) out of Maralal on the increasingly rough road to Lake Turkana (formerly Rudolf) you come upon one of the most spectacular views in Africa: the Losiolo escarpment, overlooking the Rift Valley and its volcanic moonscape. If in doubt about finding this escarpment, engage the services of a local guide at Maralal. The main road north from Maralal continues a bruising 304 km (190 miles) to Loiyangalani (see below). The journey by road should be undertaken only by well-equipped expeditions with four-wheel drive. This is the route taken by the Turkana bus and other overland expeditions to the lake (see Safaris and Transport section). Passengers normally camp at Maralal and at South Horr en route.

Isiolo, Samburu National Reserve, Buffalo Springs Reserve

The Great North Road is tarmac as far as Isiolo, descending a total of over 4,000 ft from Timau. As already mentioned, the turn-off to Wilderness Trails is on the left (page 75). Isiolo is an administrative centre and army base with no hotel accommodation. At the police check point you have to state your destination. If it is far north – that is to say not the Samburu Reserve or Wamba, but towards Marsabit – then you have to wait until a convoy with an armed guard leaves, which is normally every two days. The northbound convoys leave on Mondays, Wednesdays and Friday at around 11.00. They return from Marsabit on Tuesdays, Thursdays and Sundays. In an emergency it may be possible to find a bed at the Mission, but it is easier to go to one of the lodges in the Samburu Reserve. The dirt road on from Isiolo is liable to be corrugated and bumpy.

The Samburu National Reserve is one of the best known game viewing areas in northern Kenya. Its 225 sq km (87 sq miles) lie along the north bank of the wide Uaso Nyiro River, west of the main road, while the Buffalo Springs National Reserve of 339 sq km (130 sq miles) partially adjoins it on the south bank. The major, central, part of both reserves is fairly open thorn bush, extremely dry much of the year, thick with grass after the rains. The big attraction for game is the river, lined with a thick belt of trees including picturesque doum palms, though the water itself is muddy brown. Crocodiles sun themselves on the sandbanks – and also move a lot faster to snap at prey than one would think possible. As well as elephant, buffalo, waterbuck and other frequently seen game, there are several northern specialities such as the long necked gerenuk, a gazelle which reaches up to feed off thorn bushes, reticulated giraffe, Grevy's zebra and oryx, with long straight horns and distinctive dark markings. The most rewarding game runs are along the roads and tracks near the river and particularly at the swamp and famous clear pools of Buffalo Springs, where unhappily the large pool has been enclosed with a stone wall to keep out crocodiles. The roads away from the river to the hills in the north are particularly poor.

There are four entrances to these two reserves. Coming from Nairobi the most convenient entrance if you are going to the lodges is the Ngare Mara gate. You turn off the main road 20 km (12 miles) beyond Isiolo to the Buffalo Springs Reserve. Another gate is three km (two miles) short of Archer's Post, and is called the Buffalo Springs Gate. The Archer's Post Gate into the Samburu Reserve is reached from the township on a bad road. However you pass several Samburu *manyattas* en route. Finally the West Gate Road leads eventually to Wamba.

The two lodges are close to the bridge which crosses the Uaso Nyiro in the centre of the area. The Samburu Game Lodge (Class A, bookings Box 47557 Nairobi, telephone 335807) is run by Block Hotels and is on the north bank of the river with an aptly named Crocodile Bar close to the water. The rooms are unusually spacious for a lodge and each has a proper bathroom. The food is excellent. There is a pool and game drives are organised by UTC vehicles at Shs 690/- per vehicle. The shop sells maps of the reserves and you can get petrol – a point worth noting up here. The newer River Lodge (Class B, bookings Box 59749 Nairobi, telephone 335900) is on a more open stretch of the river, outside the Reserve on the south bank. As at Samburu Lodge, lights illuminate the game at night. There is a large swimming pool and at the time of writing substantial improvements were being made. Both lodges are 15 minutes drive from the new airstrip. Additionally there is the Buffalo Springs Tented Lodge (Class A, bookings Box 30471 Nairobi, telephone 336976) and several camp sites, which can be booked through the Park Warden. Security cannot be guaranteed at these camp sites.

Shaba National Reserve
On the other side of the Great North Road, protecting a more scenically beautiful and much less opened-up area along the south bank of the Uaso Nyiro, is the Shaba National Reserve of 362 sq km (140 sq miles). It was here that Joy Adamson re-introduced her leopard Penny to the wild and here that she was mysteriously murdered in 1980. Shaba takes its name from the copper colour of the sandstone hills, especially Mount Shaba (5,322 ft) which is partly inside the Reserve. Access is by a turn-off two km south of Archer's Post. You pass a new Game Department anti-poaching unit HQ, then traverse a long lava flow before reaching the Natorbe Gate, seven km (four miles) from the road. The Gate is open 06.30 to 18.30. From here the airstrip is to the left and so is the Shaba Tented Camp. Straight ahead is the main Reserve road running east, which is usable by ordinary cars, though the river tracks off it definitely are not. Initially the country is savannah, dotted with thorn bushes, becoming acacia woodland as you approach Mount Shaba, beyond which is wide grassy plain. Joy Adamson's camp was by Turkana hill in the centre of this plain. She christened the 40 ft waterfall at the extreme north east corner of the Reserve 'Penny's Drop'. The spring, one of many in Shaba, cascades down on to a sandbank of the river. This and the central river gorge are the two places where visitors are allowed to walk, but beware of crocodiles, which take more human lives in Kenya than any other predator.

Shaba is characterised by areas of lava flow, which came from the Nyambeni hills some 5,000 years ago, and are the reason for needing four-wheel drive in much of the Reserve. Although Shaba has a poor reputation for game viewing (because the animals are completely wild and suffer from poaching), in one morning the author saw several herds of elephant, buffalo and oryx, gerenuk, baboons, waterbuck, Grant's gazelle and many of the 280 species of birds on record, such as lilac breasted rollers. There are also leopard, lion, cheetah and hippo. After the rains in November and April the hillsides bloom with thousands of tiny flowers.

The Shaba Tented Camp (unclassified, bookings Bunson's, Box 45456 Nairobi, telephone 21992) deserves more recognition. Sheltered by trees on the river bank at a point where a clear spring runs down, creating a natural rock swimming pool, it has fully equipped tents with adjoining flush toilets, traditional makuti roofed bar and dining room and a pleasant atmosphere. Lord Lichfield used it as the base for shooting the photographs for a much publicised Firestone calendar. A vehicle is available for game drives. There are also camp sites which can be booked through the Park Warden.

Shaba to Meru via Magado

At the north east corner of the Reserve is an unmanned entrance via which you can drive in about four and a half hours to the Meru National Park, passing Chanler's Falls and the curious Magado Crater Lake. There are soda deposits in its centre, mined by the local Meru people, while the sweet water at the edges attracts nomadic Boran to bring their camels and stock to drink.

Camel Safaris

The Samburu country has long been the scene for camel safaris. Julian McKeand, a former game warden, runs first class ones from Lewa Downs near Isiolo, going up to the Uaso Nyiro west of the reserves. On average 12 clients are attended by 19 camp staff, including trackers, and 26 camels. It is a magnificent way of seeing the wild, though it involves a lot of dusty walking. McKeand also arranges much longer safaris, as far as Lake Turkana if required. He can be contacted either care of Lewa Downs (Private Bag, Isiolo) or care of Flamingo Travel (Box 45070 Nairobi).

Lolokwe and Wamba

On safari anywhere near the Uaso Nyiro you will notice the precipitiously steep, flat topped shape of Lolokwe Mountain in the distance, with the Mathews Range behind it. Lolokwe stands between the Great North Road and the fork left to Wamba. You can walk up Lolokwe's sloping northern side to find game on the top, superb views and specimens of the three most ancient trees in Africa: cycads, and the conifers *juniper* and *podocarpus*. It is beyond Archer's Post, a police post with a few *dukas*, which is the place you could hope to get petrol between Isiolo and Marsabit. Wamba itself is a colourful Samburu trading centre. The C78 dirt road past it to Maralal has been greatly improved recently. Petrol supplies at Wamba are erratic. The distance to Maralal is 164 km (102 miles) via Kisima.

On the way to Marsabit you cross the corner of the Losai National Reserve 1,806 sq km (697 sq miles), largely forest abutting on the Ndoto Hills. At the edge of the Reserve is Laisamis, on a stream, which is a pleasant spot to camp – given the savagely inhospitable nature of the lava strewn Kaisut desert beyond.

Marsabit

Marsabit is completely different from the other northern outposts, not in the tin-roofed *dukas* of the town, but in its setting. Marsabit is a 5,593 ft volcanic mountain rising green and forested out of a black lava strewn semi-desert. The area is a national reserve of 2,208 sq km (852 sq miles) noted for its large tusked elephant, reticulated giraffe and leopard. In the early evening the game comes down to drink at the crater lakes. Ahmed, once the 'king of elephants' is now dead – his replica stands at the National Museum in Nairobi. His successor, Mohammed, is reckoned to have tusks weighing more than 100 lbs each. Marsabit Lodge (Class C, bookings Box 30471 Nairobi, telephone 336976) is by one of the craters. The township has an airstrip and is about one and a half hours' flying time from Nairobi. At the time of writing it was difficult to obtain transport locally.

It is interesting to see how the tribes up here adapt to the harsh environment. Camel trains are a common sight and it's worth having a guide take you to one of the 'singing wells', the most colourful ones being at Sagante. The wells are deep so the Boran stand on scaffolds one above the other, chanting rhythmically while they pass up giraffe hide water buckets. Cows, goats and donkeys crowd around, anxious to drink.

Lake Turkana

From Marsabit an extremely rough road loops north to Lake Turkana while the more conventional route and approach is from Maralal via South Horr. The lake (formerly Rudolf) makes you feel you have walked into a *National Geographic Magazine* story. The lake itself, shimmering blue in the middle of a near desert, is savagely beautiful. Migrating wildfowl from Europe, cormorants, sacred ibis, egrets and other waterbirds flock along its shores, while pelicans fly ponderously above like flying boats on patrol. The lake is also curious. Three rivers flow into it, and none out. In fact 11 feet of water a year are taken off its 3,000 square miles by evaporation. Less explicable is why Nile perch grow to such a giant size here or indeed what geological upheaval separated the lake from the Nile aeons ago. The record perch is 375 lbs and there are also tiger fish and tilapia.

There is an oasis with an airstrip at Loiyangalani on the lake's eastern shore, where hot springs out of Mount Kulal run in a stream down to the lake. The Oasis Lodge (unclassified, bookings Ivory Safaris, Box 74609, telephone 26633) is on the site of the fishing camp where Prince Philip and Gregory Peck have stayed. It is still possible to camp nearby. The adventurous can get here by road with Safari Camp Services' seven-day bus trip, coming up via Maralal.

Close to the oasis live one of Africa's most curious tribes, the El Molo. They exist on fish, harpooned from log rafts, and the occasional hippo, and are thought to be related to the Bushmen of the Kalahari Desert in southern Africa. They number around 100: as they did when Count Teleki discovered the lake in 1888.

South Island
South Island, in the centre of the lake opposite Loiyangalani, is now a tiny national park, of 39 sq km (15 sq miles) for the benefit of ornithologists, though it can be a dangerous one to visit by boat on account of the sudden storms which blow up on the lake.

Sibiloi National Park
Some 145 km (90 miles) north of Loiyangalani lies the Sibiloi National Park; 1,570 sq km (606 sq miles) bordering the eastern shore of the lake. Besides a profusion of birds, there are herds of oryx, topi, waterbuck and other antelopes. The road from Loiyangalani to the Park is still rough, although negotiable by four-wheel drive vehicles. Camping is possible with the permission of the Warden whose office is at Alia Bay. In the park at Koobi Fora is a site explored by Richard Leakey, director of Kenya's National Museum and the son of the late Dr Louis Leakey and Mary Leakey. The site has yielded important finds, including part of a skull about 2.8 million years old that may have belonged to the first known ancestors of modern man; so this site, fertile and wooded in that long distant past, may be 'the cradle of mankind'. The skull is known by its catalogue number, '1470'. Visitors can see some of the other fossil finds in the area, including those of other hominids and of a three-toed horse, at a small museum 12 km (7 miles) from Alia Bay.

Across the western side of the lake is a magnificent natural bird sanctuary at Ferguson's Gulf. You can stay comfortably at the Lake Turkana Fishing Lodge (Class C, bookings Ivory Safaris, Box 74609 Nairobi, telephone 26633), which provides facilities for fishing, while Eliye Springs (unclassified, bookings Caspair, Box 30103 Nairobi, telephone 501938) is now only a campsite. There is an airstrip at Ferguson's Gulf, and the Fishing Lodge office can arrange flying safaris, while by land it's a two-day journey through Nakuru, Kitale and the government post of Lodwar, with its battlemented headquarters.

The Turkana themselves are as impressive as the Samburu or the Masai. Their men have their hair elaborately plaited and set with white feathers, like a coxcomb, while their necks are chokered with bead necklaces and their upper arms bound in rings of shining wire. They are nomads and almost worship their cattle. To them cattle are a man's intermediaries with his ancestors' souls; they are depended on for milk, for buying wives and for security in old age. One of the government's problems is persuading the Turkana to take them to market and exchange them for mere money.

Eastern Kenya and the Tana River

Kenya's eastern border is with the Somali Republic and its north eastern with Ethiopia. Most of the country up here is wild, semi-desert, populated by a number of nomadic tribes such as the Rendille, and including a substantial population of Somalis. The Somali government's long-standing claim to part of the North East has helped undermine security up here since well before Independence, as have the activities of *shifta*, or nomad bandits. In consequence it requires police permission to travel north east; effectively beyond the curving line of the Tana River. So Moyale on the Ethiopian border; Wajir, a Foreign legion type of outpost with white-washed and castellated buildings; and Mandera, where the three countries' frontiers meet – are all out of the question for normal tourists, although proper expeditions are allowed up to Ethiopia via Moyale. The Northern Kenya chapter covers what can be visited in that direction.

However the Tana River is the setting for a number of wildlife sanctuaries, some of which have accommodation. The Tana itself rises from sources on Mount Kenya and the Aberdares and flows some 600 km (375 miles) to the Indian Ocean, providing the water for the Seven Forks Power Station in Embu, then passing through untouched bush until reaching the Indian Ocean north of Malindi. In the 19th century, until the railway was constructed, the Tana was a route to the interior for traders and missionaries, who believed they could reach the Highlands up it, but were always defeated by rapids. Being a permanent river, its banks are lined with tall trees and other vegetation and it attracts myriad game animals and birds as well as harbouring hippos and crocodiles, while some of the country's more interesting peoples depend upon it for their agriculture. Only in 1976 was the first complete navigation of the river made.

The Meru National Park and Kora National Reserve have already been described (see page 76). To the north of the Tana, adjoining Kora, is the Rahole National Reserve, 1,270 sq km (490 sq miles) of thorn scrub around 1,000 ft above sea level, sheltering a variety of plains game, but with no tourist facilities. Down river from Rahole some 80 km (50 miles) is the trading post of Garissa where some years ago a remarkable American missionary, Brother Mario, a one-time Detroit nightclub owner, began the Garissa Boys' Town for local Somali orphans. By irrigation they have made a fruit farm in the desert round the school and their Garissa melons are famous in Kenya. The photograph of camels and goats in this guide was taken on the Tana River near Garissa and shows the thickness of the vegetation close to the banks. The Sankuri Safari Camp north of the township is now closed.

A main road (dirt) runs from Thika to Garissa and on to Somalia. Another principal road branching from it goes south all the way down to Garsen and Malindi, while a more primitive road on the eastern side eventually gets to Lamu 268 km (167 miles), passing the Arawale National Reserve on the way. This recently gazetted reserve of 533 sq km (206 sq miles) is dedicated to preserving the rare Hunter's Antelope, a hartebeest with lyre-shaped horns.

The Tana River is a major barrier, crossed by few ferries, most notably at Garissa and Garsen. By taking the main Garissa to Garsen road (238 km or

148 miles) you pass close to Hola the only important settlement on the way and gradually come into more fertile, greener country, though it is still only sparsely inhabited. A little more than half way between Hola and Garsen is the interesting Tana River Primate National Reserve.

Tana River Primate National Reserve

This 169 sq km (65 sq miles) reserve lies both sides of the Tana River near the village of Wenje and is bounded to the west by the Hola to Garsen road. It centres on a 60 km (37 mile) stretch of the little West African gallery forest to remain in East Africa and preserves its inhabitants.

There is some gallery forest in Kakemega and probably the Tana strip is the end of a forest chain running to present-day Zaire via Uganda. Certainly the Mangabey monkeys here, which are a West African species, have their nearest relatives in Zaire. The Mangabey and the Red Colobus are the two small primates which the Reserve protects. They needed protecting because of the intrusion of riverine cultivation on the forest by the local Pokomo people. Both the Mangabey and the Red Colobus are very sensitive to their environment. The highest trees in the 'gallery' are the 100 ft pale barked Tana poplars. Both trees and the dense riverine bush are alive with birds, while the river attracts game from elephant down to Red Duiker and is the home of numerous crocodiles and hippo.

The Baomo Lodge (unclassified, bookings Tana River Camp Ltd, Box 33 Malindi, telephone 270) is well situated by the river, with stone and wood bandas, each with shower and toilet. Food is basically Italian. You can see the Mangabeys and Colobus close to the camp, while boat trips reveal the full variety of wildlife. There are also good game viewing areas on the east bank. The Lodge is signed off the Garsen Road and is 158 km (99 miles) from Malindi but the roads within the Reserve are rough. Clients can also fly in to an airstrip near Wenje.

Garsen and the Tana Delta

The township of Garsen is an administrative and trading centre, mainly of tin-roofed buildings, for the Pokomo, Somalis and Orma of the area. Its ferry provides a vital link for road traffic to Lamu, but is liable to extensive flooding after the rains up country. The Delta itself is wild country, sparsely populated by the Watta tribe who were moved out of Tsavo when the park there was created. The river debouches in Ungwana (Formosa) Bay and it is nothing odd to see elephant as you fly from Malindi to Lamu, or off the road from Garsen to Lamu.

Finally, north east of Lamu, close to the frontier with the Somali Republic, are two reserves of wilderness. The Dodori National Reserve of 877 sq km (338 sq miles) can be reached by a track. Elephant and greater kudu are among the species there, while hippo can be seen at Kibukoni. The Boni National Reserve of 1,339 sq km (517 sq miles) is more easily reached by boat, though it also has an airstrip.

Southern Kenya: the Kamba, Masailand, Amboseli, Tsavo

All of the Mombasa Road's 485 km (301 miles) are tarmac. From Nairobi it leads out south east past Nairobi National Park and on to the Athi Plains. It then skirts Kitui passing close to Machakos District, where the Kamba of Wamunyu practise their traditional wood carving. These craftsmen work sitting on the ground, with legs outstretched, whittling the wood with a hoe-shaped blade called an *ngomo*. The Kamba are Kenya's third largest tribe and are also noted for being fine soldiers, and for spectacular dancing, spiced with fantastic gyrating leaps in the air and double somersaults.

The Masai

Broadly speaking the Kamba live north of the Mombasa Road, and the Masai south. The Masai's ancestral territory stretched north up the Rift and round to Laikipia and today they still herd their cattle as far west as the Mara and way down into Tanzania: the colonially established frontier divides the tribe. Within this broad ethnic grouping, there are distinct Masai communities, for instance those in the Mara are different to those centred on Loitokitok. However they all share the same legendary warrior tradition. The young *moran*, or warrior, athletic, aquiline-featured, his hair braided and thickened with red ochre, looks like a figure off a classical Greek vase as he stands leaning on his spear. His traditional stories are folk epics of lion hunts and he grows up believing that they are told only at night because if you waste time telling stories during the day you will go blind. Like the Turkana *moran*, he lives by and for his cattle. The traditional Masai food is blood mixed with milk and curdled, the blood itself being expertly taken from the jugular vein in a cow's neck without injuring the beast. Most Masai still live nomadically, building their *manyattas* wherever there is grazing. A *manyatta* is a group of low huts made of dung and surrounded by a thorn fence, inside which the cattle are brought at night for protection. You see them everywhere in Masailand, often abandoned because the herdsmen have moved on to new pastures.

The 1979 census recorded 240,000 Masai in Kenya, while numerous books detail their lives and the important ceremonies which punctuate their existence, such as the *Emorata*, or circumcision and the traumatic *Eunoto*, when the warrior's mothers shave off their long, plaited hair in token of their progressing to elderhood and marriage. A magnificent pictorial account of the tribe, written by a Masai, is *Maasai* by Tepilit Ole Saitoti, with photographs by Carol Beckwith. (Purists sometimes spell the word with two 'a's.) The traditionally noble Masai is a far cry from the opportunist men and women who today besiege tourist buses outside Amboseli.

Amboseli National Park

Amboseli, lying almost in the shadow of Mount Kilimanjaro, is part of an important Masai district. To reach it by road you turn off the Nairobi to Mombasa A109 at Athi River on to the A104 to Kajiado, Namanga and Arusha in Tanzania, which is a good fast tarmac road. Kajiado is a small township of tin-roofed *dukas*. Nearby are the quarries producing Kenya's marble. Namanga is the frontier post, 135 km (84 miles) from Nairobi. Remember the frontier is closed unless you have official Tanzanian permission to cross. From Namanga a reasonable road runs through the Namanga Gate of

Amboseli into the Reserve and so to the Park. The Namanga Hotel (unclassified, telephone Namanga 4) is like a game lodge in character and has a pool, though it lacks the quality of other lodges in the area.

The Namanga entrance to Amboseli is the most popular. The alternative is to drive down the Mombasa Road to Sultan Hamud, from where a straight well-graded dirt road runs south and passes Amboseli going on to Loitokitok. You can either turn off at Makutano for the Lemi Boti Gate or go further and enter the Park at the Kimana Gate.

Before the 1,235 sq miles of the Amboseli Game Reserve had their most vital 146 sq miles designated as a national park, the Masai shared the area with the game which they seldom kill for meat, being preoccupied with their cattle. But there was not pasture for both and under an agreement with the government the Masai moved out after a pipeline had been constructed to bring water from outside the Park. However the Park's boundaries have had to be further reduced and in times of drought you will still see Masai herding cattle and goats within the Park. Amboseli's landscape is dominated by Mount Kilimanjaro to the south, though its snowcapped summit is often shrouded by cloud and it is most likely to be seen either early or late in the day. People commonly look too low down on the horizon for it. Remember it is 19,340 ft high. Seen from Amboseli the main summit, Kibo (Uhuru Peak), is on the right while the sharper peak of Mawenzi (16,900 ft) is on the left.

Although there is game to be seen in most parts of the Reserve, organised tours concentrate on the Park, almost at the centre of which are the airfield, the Park Headquarters at Ol Tukai and the main lodges (see below). To the west is Lake Amboseli, optimistically marked blue on maps, but in practice a dry bed of soda most of the year, which produced mirages like a desert. There are tracks across it, though if it has rained your vehicle will sink through the surface. Kongoni and eland are among animals that frequent the lake area.

However most of Amboseli's game is drawn to the swamps and permanent water in the centre and south of the Park. The Loginye swamp east and north of Ol Tukai is fed by natural springs, is green all the year and attracts a lot of game in dry weather. The zebra and wildebeest congregate here, pursued by lion; elephant move in and there are a number of rhino. Loginye is uncrossable in the rains. The other swamp is the Enkongo Narok to the south, where you will find waterbuck, buffalo, elephant and a multitude of birds. Between the two swamps is the Empash area, once forested but now losing its trees due to the depredations of elephants and the rising salinity in the earth.

A causeway road crosses one arm of the Enkongo Narok swamp and leads round to Observation Hill, or Enamishera Hill, a knoll perhaps 100 ft high on which there is a viewing hut. Elephant often congregate in the swamp below and you can get an idea of the whole Park, since it is almost completely flat.

Other animals that can be seen, though you need a guide, include caracal, cheetah, civet cat and serval cat; gerenuk up near Lemi Boti, oryx, impala and giraffe. Leopard like the trees along the southern boundary towards Kitirua. Pelicans, herons and jacanas are among the many waterbirds.

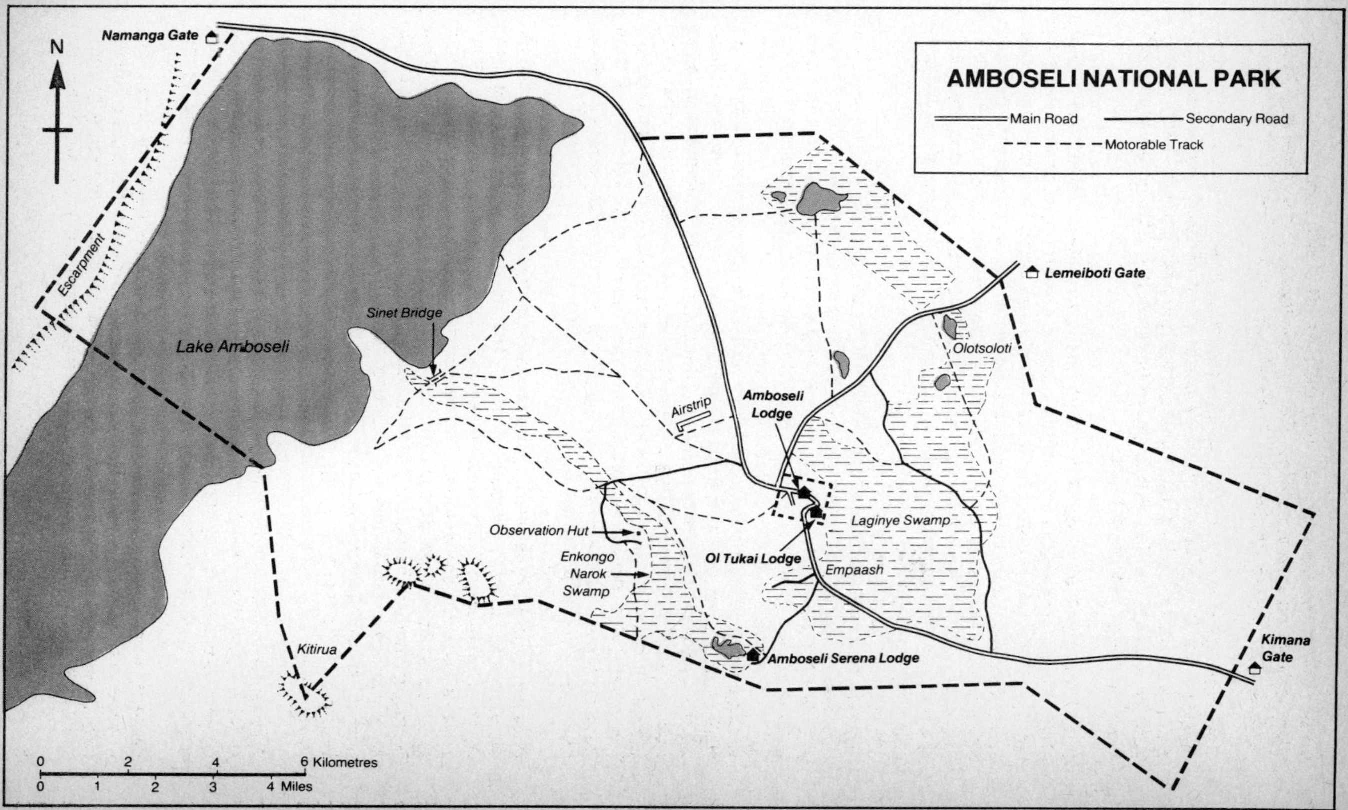
AMBOSELI NATIONAL PARK
Main Road
Secondary Road
Motorable Track
N
Namanga Gate
Escarpment
Lake Amboseli
Sinet Bridge
Airstrip
Amboseli Lodge
Lemeiboti Gate
Olotsoloti
Laginye Swamp
Ol Tukai Lodge
Empaash
Observation Hut
Enkongo Narok Swamp
Amboseli Serena Lodge
Kitirua
Kimana Gate
0 2 4 6 Kilometres
0 1 2 3 4 Miles

Accommodation in the Park has recently been increased. The best situated is the very comfortable Amboseli Serena Lodge (Class A, bookings Box 46860 Nairobi, telephone 338656). It stands alongside the Enkongo Narok swamp so that you get good game viewing both from the verandahs and from the rooms and is built in a style derived from traditional Masai *manyattas*. Close to Ol Tukai is the Amboseli New Lodge (Class B) and near it the former tented camp has been rebuilt as the Kilimanjaro Safari Club (Class C, bookings for both at Box 30139 Nairobi, telephone 27136). The cheapest rooms are in the self-service bandas at Ol Tukai, which have good facilities including gas cooking and a shop. Bookings through Let's Go Travel (Box 60342 Nairobi, telephone 29539). The campsite has been moved outside the southern boundary of the Park some 3 km (2 miles) from Observation Hill and is well signed. It is run by the Masai Group Ranch and you book on arrival at an office near the southern boundary, which is equally well signed. Close to the Park's eastern boundary outside the gate is the Kilimanjaro Buffalo Lodge (Class A, bookings Box 72630 Nairobi, telephone 336088). This is the newest establishment with rooms in luxurious rondavels, a pool and conference facilities.

Amboseli to Tsavo and the Chyulu Hills

From Amboseli it is possible to drive direct to the western part of the Tsavo National Park, a distance of approximately 80 km (50 miles), though the dirt road is extremely rough in places. You leave Amboseli by the Kimana Gate, go briefly down the C102 road to Loitokitok, then turn left again. Loitokitok itself is a Masai township, 8,000 ft up on the slopes of Kilimanjaro. It is along the road to Tsavo that the local Masai can be so obstructive. We have experienced them physically blocking the road in order to demand money for *piksha* (photographing them). The only answer is to drive firmly on, unless you want to be completely beseiged. Within Tsavo Park, before reaching the gate, you drive across the edge of the Shetani lava flow at the foot of the Chyulu Hills. The road surface is appropriately bad. The lava itself, still black and almost untouched by vegetation, is worth stopping to see. It derived from an eruption some 200 years ago which is vividly remembered in Masai folk tales. The Chyulu Hills themselves rise to 7,248 ft and are a good place to camp as you wish. The views are splendid and there is a lot of wildlife, plus a network of caves. The only snag – and the reason they are undisturbed by man – is the lack of water. So take plenty. The normal approach to the hills is taking the C102 from Sultan Hamud on the Mombasa Road and turning right at Makutano, though there are ways in to the range from Mtito Andei, which brings us back to the Mombasa Road and the better known entrances to Tsavo.

Nairobi direct to the Tsavo National Park

The Mombasa Road is a fast one. You should reach Mtito Andei entrance to Tsavo West National Park (236 km or 148 miles) in two and a half hours. You will notice small distance signs every two km, which are marked with abbreviations of place names. Thus 'Msa' stands for Mombasa and 'Nbi' for Nairobi. There are several places to stop the night or eat en route to the coast. At Makindu, 145 km (90 miles) where there is a petrol station, is the Hunter's Lodge (Class D, bookings Box 67868 Nairobi, telephone 21439), more attractive than its classification suggests as it is set by a small lake and is well furnished. Snacks are served on the terrace. This used to be a base for hunting in the Chyulu and there are some interesting caves not far off. Further on at Kibwezi is the left turn-off to reach a self-service lodge, the Bushwhackers Camp (address PO Kibwezi) on the border of Tsavo East. Mtito Andei is the recognised half way house to the coast, with several service stations and snack bars, as well as the Tsavo Inn (Class D, bookings Kilimanjaro Safari Club, Box 30139 Nairobi, telephone 27136) which has a restaurant and a swimming pool. The Inn is opposite the main gate to the Park and if you stay there you often hear the lions roaring at night.

Tsavo National Park

The Tsavo National Park is roughly kidney shaped and its 21,000 sq km (8,100 sq miles) are bisected in the middle by the Mombasa Road. For administrative convenience the part north east of the road is called Tsavo East, with a headquarters near Voi and the part south west of the road is Tsavo West, with Wardens' offices near Mtito Andei. Overall this famous national park covers a vast section of the 200 miles of thorn scrub, spiked with the bulbous trunks of baobab trees, that separate the tropical vegetation of the coast from the great central plateau of the African continent.

It was the endless thorn scrub here that kept the peoples of the interior remote from western civilisation for so many centuries. Try walking through it as the early missionaries did and you will soon understand. It has various names – the Nyika, which means thorn country, the Nyiri Desert, the Taru Desert. Much of the year it is burnt dry and dusty by the sun. Then overnight the rains transform it. Convolvulus flowers burst out white and purple, grass seed germinates, the bushes are suddenly green. Explorers hated it for the very reason that makes it a major attraction today – the game. 'Full of wild beasts, such as rhinoceros, buffaloes and elephants', the German missionary, Rebmann, noted in his diary on May 11, 1848. Indeed it is full, though over grazing has depleted the vegetation in parts and the elephant population is now only an estimated 15,000 to 20,000. They are fairly accustomed to cars, but if you meet one on the road drive cautiously.

Tsavo's lions are noted for their ferocity. J. H. Patterson's book, *The Man Eaters of Tsavo,* describes how they obstructed the building of the railway in the 1900s by the simple expedient of eating the linesmen. The railway carriage from which a lion dragged a man is displayed in the Railway Museum in Nairobi. Nowadays they seem to prefer the eland, kongoni, impala, klipspringer, kudu, reedbuck, waterbuck and Burchell's zebra which also inhabit the Park. Humans are apparently an acquired taste.

Tsavo West National Park

In Tsavo West, which is rather hilly, the volcanic area where the Mzima Springs and other waters rise attracts most species of game. The Springs, 40 km (25 miles) from Mtito Andei, form a series of clear pools fed by a flow estimated at 50 million gallons a day, coming underground from Kilimanjaro. This oasis attracts many animals and an observation tank in the top pool enables you to watch hippo and crocodile from underwater. Other major viewing places are at the Kangethwa Dam, the Kilaguni waterhole and an artificial spring right in front of the Kilaguni Lodge verandah, where a sign reads 'Animals are requested to be quiet whilst guests are drinking, and vice versa.'

There are three lodges near Mzima Springs. Kilaguni Lodge (Class A, bookings Box 30471 Nairobi, telephone 336858) is justifiably renowned. It has its own airstrip, swimming pool and reasonably priced game park tours. A short drive east of the Springs is the Ngulia Safari Lodge built on the edge of the Ndawe escarpment with a magnificent view over vast plains. There is a swimming pool in the grounds, and an airstrip a short distance away. It is classed A, bookings as for Kilaguni. Nearby is Ngulia Safari Camp, on a site 'haunted' by lions which leave no footprints, according to local legend. You must bring food and bedding. Kitani Lodge, west of Mzima Springs, is also self-service, though bedding can be hired and there is a food shop. Both are cheap and you book through AA Travel (Box 14982 Nairobi, telephone 720382). There is also a campsite near the Chyulu gate.

As the map shows, the above area is only a small part of Tsavo West's expanse. The Park stretches much further south into a part known as the Serengeti Plains, or the Little Serengeti, which is being increasingly opened up. The name is confusing. These plains have nothing to do with the Serengeti National Park far away in Tanzania, though it is similar country. It is crossed by the meandering road and railway from Voi to Taveta, in the shadow of Mount Kilimanjaro, both of which continue across the frontier to Moshi. Half way across is the abandoned ghost town of Murka, while both along here and up in the shallow valley of the Tsavo River there are reminders of a curious piece of history. The railway line was built by the British during World War 1 to bring supplies to the front against the Germans, who had colonised Tanganyika. The British chased the German Commander, General Paul von Lettow-Vorbeck, and his troops all the way through what are today Tanzania, Mozambique, Zambia and back into Tanzania without capturing them; they finally surrendered in 1918 on hearing of the Kaiser's capitulation in Europe. The story is well told in Charles Miller's *Battle for the Bundu*. The high ground north off the Tsavo River was one British defensive line against the initial German attack and astonishingly traces of the war are still to be found there, including empty whisky bottles!

Close to the Tanzania border, south of the road, is Lake Jipe, a paradise for water birds, among rarities being pygmy goose. There is a self-service camp and a motorboat can be hired. Similarly close to the frontier, but north of the road and reached by a turn-off before Taveta, is the surprising Lake Chala, a circular crater lake full of crocodiles which is coloured green by minerals. Both lakes are accessible by dirt roads.

Two excellent lodges serving the central part of Tsavo West are situated close to the Voi – Taveta road in the Taita Hills. Both are run by Hilton Hotels (Box 30624 Nairobi, telephone 334000). The Taita Hills Lodge (Class A) supposedly resembles a World War 1 fort, but this curious idea does not detract from its comfort. Salt Lick Lodge has rooms like higher versions of traditional African thatched huts mounted on stilts to give a view over a large waterhole, a design which is more intriguing than it sounds. The waterhole and salt licks attract as many as 500 buffalo in the evenings and this is also a good area for seeing lion. Both lodges have airstrips and pools and organise trips into the Taita Hills where there is a mysterious 'cave of skulls' as well as Lakes Chala and Jipe.

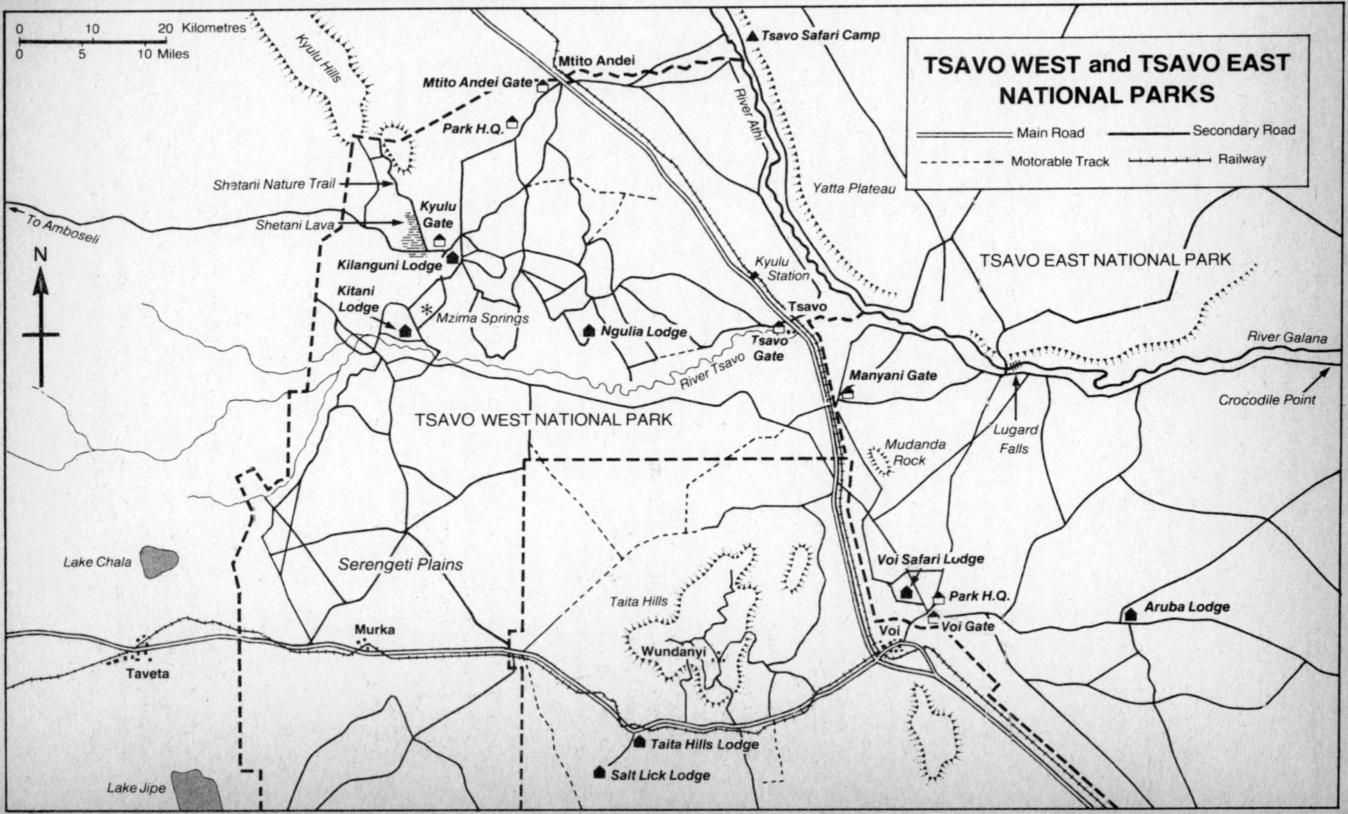

TSAVO WEST and TSAVO EAST NATIONAL PARKS
Main Road
Secondary Road
Motorable Track
Railway
0 10 20 Kilometres
0 5 10 Miles
N
Kyulu Hills
Mtito Andei
Mtito Andei Gate
Park H.Q.
Tsavo Safari Camp
River Athi
Yatta Plateau
Shetani Nature Trail
Shetani Lava
To Amboseli
Kyulu Gate
Kilanguni Lodge
Kitani Lodge
Mzima Springs
Ngulia Lodge
Kyulu Station
Tsavo
Tsavo Gate
River Tsavo
TSAVO EAST NATIONAL PARK
River Galana
Crocodile Point
Manyani Gate
Lugard Falls
Mudanda Rock
TSAVO WEST NATIONAL PARK
Lake Chala
Serengeti Plains
Taita Hills
Voi Safari Lodge
Park H.Q.
Aruba Lodge
Voi
Voi Gate
Murka
Wundanyi
Taveta
Taita Hills Lodge
Salt Lick Lodge
Lake Jipe

Taita Hills and Voi
The Taita Hills, between Tsavo West and Voi, are steep and fertile, while the Taita people are friendly and it can be fun to explore their villages and markets. The road up to Wundanyi climbs 3,000 ft in a few kilometres giving very varied views. The township of Voi is only 1,800 ft up and appreciably hotter than Nairobi, though the nights are cool. It has the usual *dukas* but is not a tourist shopping centre. You pass through Voi to reach the Voi gate to Tsavo East; though the Park has a gate further north at Manyani, as well as access via Mtito Andei to a safari camp on the Athi River.

Tsavo East National Park
Tsavo East is less hilly than Tsavo West, apart from the dramatic line of the Yatta Plateau escarpment which rises almost parallel to the Mombasa Road and in origin is a lava flow. Beyond this escarpment, to the east, is a seemingly endless expanse of low lying semi-desert, spiked with thorn bushes, most of which you can only visit by special permission of the Park Warden. All roads north of the Galana River, which cuts across Tsavo East, are closed to the public. Lugard Falls and Crocodile Point on the river are worth a visit, though the best places to see animals are unquestionably Mudanda Rock and Aruba. The former is a great hump of rusty coloured rock overlooking a huge waterhole making a natural amphitheatre. It is signed off the park road between the Manyani gate and the Voi gate and you can leave your car to climb up.

The Voi Safari Lodge, along this road, is ingeniously set on the Worsessa look-out hill above the plain and a small waterhole. (Class A, bookings Box 30471 Nairobi, telephone 336858.) The Aruba Dam, pretty well in the centre of this part of the park, is a successful man-made watering place for game. The self-help Aruba Lodge is run by the Ministry of Tourism and Wildlife (bookings AA Travel, Box 40087 Nairobi, telephone 720382). Finally, five km outside the Sala gate on the Galana River, is the Crocodile Tented Camp (class B), haunt of the reptiles. It is on the road to Malindi and is owned by the Eden Roc Hotel (Box 350 Malindi, telephone 20480). Set under thorn trees by the river, this is a good place to stop if you are driving direct from the Park to Malindi, which is 95 km (60 miles) further on (see below).

Further up in Tsavo East on the east bank of the Athi River – which becomes the Galana at the southern end of the Yatta escarpment, where the Tsavo River joins it – is the semi-permanent Tsavo Tented Safari Camp (class B, bookings Box 30139 Nairobi, telephone 27136). The dirt road from Mtito Andei goes to the opposite bank of the river and you are then taken across. The camp has its own airstrip and runs its own hunting cars for game drives. We saw many elephant, rhino, buffalo, waterbuck, giraffe, warthog, various antelope – and no other cars – on our trip along the river banks. You must have a pass or accommodation voucher before entering this part of the Park.

Remember you must be into your lodge by 19.00 which means being at the park gates considerably earlier. Also note that midday temperatures down here reach 90° to 100°F, which is too hot for both animals and sightseers – so early morning and early evening are the times for game viewing.

Tsavo to Malindi and the Galana Game Ranch
Although the vast eastern side of Tsavo is bleak, bordering on the Taru Desert, and has been heavily poached by ivory hunters, the dirt road from Manyani to Malindi along the south bank of the Galana is well worth taking if you are not in a hurry. You need four-wheel drive in the rains, the driving time from Sala to Malindi being two hours or so. After leaving the Sala gate the road takes a reasonably direct route, sometimes close to the river. Seven km (four miles) from the gate and two km from Crocodile Camp is the left turn-off to the largest ranch in Kenya, the 1½-million-acre Galana Game Ranch, which is reached by a three km road to the river, crossing a causeway and checking in at the guarded barrier. The ranch has a private lodge, each banda style room having its own shower and lavatory, and is pleasantly set on a bluff above the river. Overall it is a completely self-contained safari area, 1,500 ft above sea level, with tree game viewing platforms and many species of plains game sharing its immense territory with 21,000 head of cattle. Night game drives, camel safaris and bird watching are amongst the activities that can be organised. Some imaginative experiments in ranching game have been tried here and there is a herd of domesticated oryx. It is associated with Sangare Ranch near Mweiga and with the Indian Ocean Lodge at Malindi (see North Coast chapter) from which it is 30 minutes flying time. Enquiries to Galana Game and Ranching Ltd (Box 76 Malindi).

Continuing along the Malindi Road, the bush gradually becomes thicker until some 40 km (25 miles) from the town you enter the completely different vegetation of the coastal strip, including palm trees and mango and cashew nut trees. The road cuts through a corner of the Jilore Forest and past the airfield to Malindi, described later.

The Coast

The Kenya coast is a series of long bays between coral headlands, punctuated by occasional river creeks running for 480 km (300 miles) from Somalia to Tanzania, though the northern extremity is little visited because it is so inaccessible. It is lined with waving palm trees, mangoes, casuarinas and gorgeously flowering hibiscus, oleander, frangipani and bougainvillaea. The beaches are great sweeps of white coral sand, while about a kilometre out in the Indian Ocean runs a coral reef protecting almost the whole length of the shore from sharks and creating a series of lagoons where the water is crystal clear and an enormous variety of tropical fish feed on the coral. The skin-diving – known locally as goggling – rivals the Caribbean's, and so does the big game fishing. Overall it would make a superb backdrop to a James Bond story.

The Reef
The story behind the reef and its teeming fish is both simple and unexpected. The Continental shelf is narrow, descending sharply to considerable depths only three to eight kilometres from the beach (two to five miles), and reef building corals cannot survive below 45 metres. Therefore the reef, usually several parallel reefs in fact, is close inshore. Furthermore corals like warm, clear, saline water. So there is always a break in the reef where rivers like the Sabaki bring down cooler, muddy, fresh water, for instance at Malindi, Kilifi and Mombasa. The coral itself is made up of the hard, calcareous skeletons of countless tiny polyps, growing one upon the other. What is

surprising is that the fish living along the reef, feeding on the coral – angel fish, parrot fish and myriad others – originated in the South Pacific. They were brought to Africa by the South Equatorial Current, which flows continuously east to west, then carried to Kenya's coast by the East African Coastal Current running north from Mozambique. A useful reference book on them is *A Guide to the Common Reef Fishes of the Western Indian Ocean*, by K. Bock, published by Macmillan Education Ltd, London.

Skindiving along the reef to observe the fish, sponges, anenomes, crabs and starfish that live there is easy: all you need is a rubber mask or snorkel, with flippers or tennis shoes. But beware of the poisonous mottled brown stonefish and of spiny black sea urchins. Both can cause seriously infected wounds. Even worse are the depredations caused to the reef by shell collectors and coral hunters selling to tourists and threatening the life of the reef. To save it the export of shells has been banned since 1979.

Big Game Fishing

Big game fishing centres dot the coast: Malindi, Watamu, Kilifi and Shimoni, to name only the major ones. Catches often make records. One Mako shark caught off the coast weighed 325 kg. Returning fishing boats sport flags to denote their successes: yellow for shark, red for sailfish, black for black marlin, blue for blue marlin, green for striped marlin, varying colours for wahoo depending on the location. For enthusiasts these safaris into the ocean are as exciting as any on land.

The fishing, the reef, above all the superb coral beaches and the average of ten hours sunshine a day, have made the Kenya coast into an international playground. Half of the country's best hotels are at the coast and many visitors never go up-country at all. This has bad effects on local culture and traditions, which were particularly strong and ancient here.

History

The ancient Greeks called the coast 'Azania', the 'dry country' and Ptolemy, the great Egyptian geographer marked Mombasa on his maps as Tonike around AD 160. More than a thousand years ago Arab traders and conquerors from Oman sailed south in their dhows, bringing Islamic religion and its culture, which are still predominant today despite the later influence of Chinese, Portuguese and British explorers, traders and colonists. All down the coast lie the mouldering remains of the Arab Sultanates established here from about AD 900 onwards. Surprisingly their tenure only officially ended on Kenya's and Zanzibar's Independence, when the Sultan of Zanzibar, subsequently deposed, surrendered his legal right to the 10 miles wide 'coastal strip'. The British had recognised this claim throughout their rule of the two countries. The Arab colonisers exported ivory, Ethiopian gold, leopard skins and rhino horn from the interior, and also slaves, a practice that has left its mark on Arab-African relationships today, even though the slave trade was put down by the British in the 1870s. However, Arab culture has also imparted a well-mannered, unhurried aura to the coastal way of life. Indeed Arab intermarriage with the Giriama, Bajun and other African coastal tribes produced the Swahili people and their language, which has spread to become the lingua franca of all eastern Africa. Links with Arabia are still maintained by the dhow fleets that ply down to Mombasa and Dar es Salaam on the north east monsoon, the Kaskasi, in January; and return to the Arabian Gulf and India in May on the south east monsoon, the Kuzi.

Climate

The coast's climate is tropical. February and March are the warmest months (86°F (31°C) mean maximum temperature) but really it's the relative humidity of 75 that one notices, so April and November, when the wind is slack, can seem the hottest. The cooler season from July to mid-December is when many local people think the coast climate is at its best. It's advisable to take anti-malarial pills: see also General Information.

Mombasa

Kenya's second town, the largest port on this coast north of Durban, Mombasa is strictly speaking an island, connected to the mainland by the Makupa Causeway, which carries both the famous railway and the modern road. Moi International Airport is on the mainland side of the causeway, some 20 minutes drive from the city centre. Kenya Airways operates two or more flights a day to Mombasa, the flying time being one hour from Nairobi and less than half an hour from Malindi. By road the 485 km (301 miles) take five or six hours, depending whether you stop en route. The express bus fare is only Shs 100/-. Even so, hitch-hiking is common, though it presents a slight risk of being beaten up and robbed. As already explained in the Transport and Safaris section, the overnight train is good value.

Mombasa has a long and proud history. Identifiable as a port in a sailing guide to the Indian Ocean called *The Periplus of the Erythraean Sea* published in Alexandria AD 80, it became one of the principal settlements of Arabs from the Oman and Muscat who colonised the East Africa coast and who gave such a hostile reception to the first European to land here, Vasco da Gama, that the renowned Portuguese explorer sailed on to Malindi. Nonetheless Portuguese warships followed in his wake and the occupation of Mombasa which resulted was only ended when the Arabs recaptured the port in the 18th century. From then on the town and port remained a key possession of the Sultan of Muscat's empire until he transferred his court to Zanzibar in 1832. The opening of the railway in 1901 revived Mombasa as the gateway to East Africa, though the Sultan of Zanzibar's plain red flag continued to fly in Mombasa by courtesy of the British until Independence in 1963.

The Old Town

The Arab influence at the coast is most clearly visible in Mombasa and the far smaller port of Lamu, also an island, further north. However it is more relaxed in Mombasa, because this is one of the world's great cross roads, the meeting place of traders from many nations. By far the most fascinating part of Mombasa is the Old Town, which lies between Makadara Road and the old harbour (see map). Its narrow streets are overshadowed by high houses with elaborately carved ornamental balconies. Itinerant Arabs sell coffee from traditional long-beaked copper pots. Oriental music drifts out from the shops of moneylenders, goldsmiths, tinsmiths, tailors, makers of sweetmeats and other traders, mostly Asian. Oriental mosques and temples, like the new Jain Temple, its pillars and domes as white as icing on a gargantuan wedding cake, jostle for space with bustling African markets and stalls. Everywhere there is hustle, life and a multitude of languages. Mombasa, in fact, has the same cosmopolitan feeling as Hong Kong, Singapore and other world ports. Both old and new parts deserve a visit.

To find the old harbour go down Nkrumah Road, past the interesting old Treasury Square with its monuments, and past Fort Jesus. The street becomes Mbaraki Hinawy Road and leads past alleyways to the tiny Government Square and the Customs Landing Stage. Between January and March you can be shown round the dhows. For a few shillings a boatman will row you out to one. The *Nahoda*, the dhow captain, will usually welcome a visitor with coffee, black and bitter, from a tiny cup, and may well have fine carpets and Arab chests for sale among his cargo. Dhows and other boats sail up the coast to Lamu and with some discomfort you could take passage in one.

The shops around Government Square offer carpets, Arab chests, brasswork and carvings. Nearby is Yusuf Jaffer's Perfume Shop, where exotically named scents line the walls. They are made without alcohol, which means they do not evaporate (and persist for weeks if you don't bathe!). His shop sign says it all: '. . . the right and real non-alcoholic perfumes super power natural flowers. 300 varieties with sandalwood oil . . .' At another shop the sign announces 'Dealers in carpets, bedsheets, Arab chests, toys, folding bags, non-alcoholic perfumes, pure leather slippers.' Although you might expect these back streets to be squalid and even dangerous, they are neither, and considerably more entertaining to stroll around than the curio stalls which line Moi Avenue along from its junction with Digo Road, where you will be constantly pestered to buy. While in the Old Town make a point of going to the Old Port Tourist shop in Government Square, which among many things sells batiks, amber jewellery and Ethiopian silverwork.

It's worth paying a few shillings for one of the Old Town's numerous self-appointed guides. Get him to show you the cliff west of Government Square, down through which a flight of steps leads to a cave with a well, where the slaving dhows used to take on water secretly. Mombasa was an important staging post in the inhuman business of taking African slaves from all over the interior of East Africa to the slave market in Zanzibar: a market which was only closed in 1873. Frere Town, outside Mombasa to the north, was created at the instigation of Sir Bartle Frere to house freed slaves (see below). Even today the horrors of the slave trade are still remembered. Your guide should take you past the stumpy white minaret of the ancient Maudhry Mosque in Mbaraki Hinawy Road

He should point out the pure Arabs in their beaded hats and embroidered cloth gowns; the Hindus whose women wear tiny gold studs in their noses and colourful silk saris; and the Swahili men who wear a long white robe, or more often a brightly printed length of cloth wrapped round the waist like a skirt and known as a *kikoi*, while the women wear *kangas*, wrapped round beneath the armpits and falling to mid-calf length. *Kangas* are brighter and gayer than *kikois* and are a real fashion bargain. They are cheap, infinitely varied and, like the useful straw sunhats made locally, you can get them all along the coast. Women of the Moslem faith modestly drape themselves from head to toe in an all-enveloping black garment called a *buibui*, Cynics, however, claim the *buibui* remains popular because it doesn't matter what

Above: Rhino and egrets
Below: Diani Beach. By Richard Cox

Above: Hippo family
Below: Crested cranes

)pposite above left: Luo elder in ribal dress
)pposite above right: Boy at Bagamayo, 'anzania
)pposite below: Uganda kob

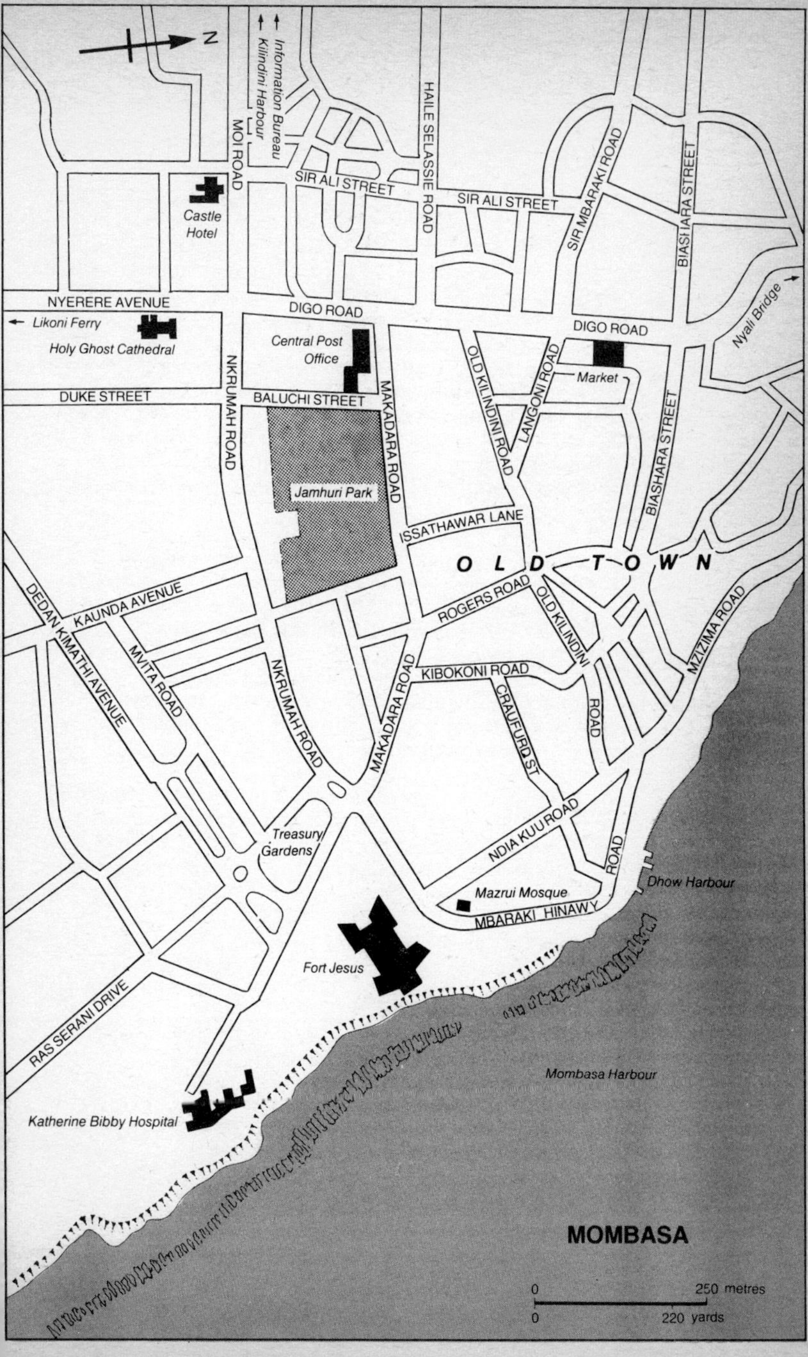

N
Information Bureau
Kilindini Harbour
MOI ROAD
HAILE SELASSIE ROAD
SIR ALI STREET
SIR ALI STREET
SIR MBARAKI ROAD
BIASHARA STREET
Castle Hotel
NYERERE AVENUE
DIGO ROAD
DIGO ROAD
Likoni Ferry
Holy Ghost Cathedral
Central Post Office
Nyali Bridge
Market
OLD KILINDINI ROAD
LANGONI ROAD
DUKE STREET
BALUCHI STREET
NKRUMAH ROAD
MAKADARA ROAD
BIASHARA STREET
Jamhuri Park
ISSATHAWAR LANE
OLD TOWN
KAUNDA AVENUE
ROGERS ROAD
OLD KILINDINI ROAD
MZIZIMA ROAD
DEDAN KIMATHI AVENUE
MVITA ROAD
NKRUMAH ROAD
KIBOKONI ROAD
CRAUFURD ST
MAKADARA ROAD
NDIA KUU ROAD
ROAD
Treasury Gardens
Dhow Harbour
Mazrui Mosque
MBARAKI HINAWY
Fort Jesus
RAS SERANI DRIVE
Mombasa Harbour
Katherine Bibby Hospital
MOMBASA
0
250 metres
0
220 yards

the wearer has on underneath, or if she has done her hair. You will see schoolgirls, compromising between tradition and modernity, with their *buibuis* thrown back to reveal their faces and their white school blouses, rather as if the garment was an academic gown, not a veil. Girls wear the *buibui* from 14 years old for the rest of their of lives.

Fort Jesus

At the north corner of the Old Town stands the Portuguese castle, Fort Jesus, weathered and immense. Its building began in 1593. A century later the Arabs took it in 1698 after a 24-month siege, though they lost it again. The Portuguese finally left in 1729. Today its guns still command the harbour, looking out beyond English Point, but the fort itself houses a comprehensive museum dealing with the culture, architecture and history of the coast. Fort Jesus is open daily and a detailed booklet about it is on sale at the entrance. Among many interesting things there are two cycads, fern-like plants which have been in existence for 200 million years, and relics salvaged from a Portuguese warship which sank near the fort. The coats of arms, carved in stone, of Portuguese commanders are worth studying. There is also a curious room of ordinary sailors *graffiti*, including drawings of the ships of their time, which show what the sunken warship may have looked like to her crew.

Outside the fort, guarding the main entrance, stand two relics of the First World War and the campaigns mentioned in the description of the Tsavo Park (see page 90). One is a 4.1 inch gun from the German cruiser, the SMS Koenigsberg, which the Royal Navy sank in the Rufiji Delta in southern Tanganyika in 1915. Ten of these guns were salvaged at the orders of the ingenious and tireless General von Lettow Vorbeck, turned into field guns, and hauled with him across the bush for many months. The other gun is a 4 inch one converted to coastal artillery use after the British cruiser HMS Pegasus was sunk by the Germans off Zanzibar in 1914.

If you take the path down to the left of the fort, it leads along beneath the battlements above the shoreline, where you can watch local fishermen casting their nets. This path is one of the best places from which to photograph the fort, which is not an easy subject. Immediately adjoining the fort is the old colonial style Mombasa Club, while on the other side there are attractive old buildings in Treasury Square. On Mvita Road, near Treasury Square, is the Wildlife Conservation and Management Department's ivory room, where elephant tusks, rhino horns and other game trophies taken from poachers or dead animals are displayed. The room is open on weekdays.

The rest of Mombasa is a modern, thriving city, basing its prosperity on Kilindini Harbour. One of the main shopping streets is Moi Avenue, formerly Kilindini Road, leading to the port, past the famous arch of giant elephant tusks (metal not ivory!) close to which is the Information Bureau (Box 85072, telephone 25428). Round here and in Digo Road and Nyerere Avenue you can buy wood carvings, curios, brass-bound Arab chests of all sizes, Indian saris, sandals, straw hats and baskets. Teadin's and Kenrocks, both in Moi Avenue, are good for gemstones. Biashara Street near the Municipal Market (itself worth a look) sells African fabrics and also Moslem caps, called *kofias* in Swahili. A visit to the African market in Mwembe Tayari, off Jomo Kenyatta Avenue, is amusing. You can buy *kikois*, *kangas*, colourful shirts of

African design and beaded hats, not to mention all the necessary herbs and relics for witchdoctoring. Medicines and photographic goods can be bought from chemists in Moi Avenue. There are several good small shops for men's clothing, shoes and tourist curios, and a Home Industries Shop which displays locally made goods.

On Moi Avenue, near the junction with Digo Road, is one of the most amusing social gathering places in the whole of Kenya: the verandah terrace of the Castle Hotel. Its patrons are an amazing mix of young 'travellers', African girls whose unabashed role is the pursuit of pleasure, sailors – especially Americans since the US Navy started enlarging the harbour entrance so that fleet carriers can enter – and holidaymakers. The *samosas* they serve here can be recommended.

Hotels

Because there no beaches in Mombasa Island, virtually all the hotel development in the area has taken place to the north and south, which we come to in a moment. The most modern hotel on Mombasa Island, and certainly the largest, used to be the Oceanic. However it has been partly converted into apartments and now has only a number of economy rooms, albeit air-conditioned, and is classed D (address Box 90371, telephone 311191). The Outrigger Hotel (Class D, Box 82345, telephone 20822) on Ras Liwatoni Road is also air-conditioned, has a pool and overlooks Kilindini Harbour. A good older hotel is the Manor (Class D, Box 84851, telephone 21821) on Nyerere Avenue. The Castle Hotel is also Class D (Box 84231, telephone 23403). Others range down to the very cheap, where you share a room. A list is published in *What's On in Kenya*. Except at the latter, it is desirable to book in advance in the high season, roughly August to March, although off-peak rates offer large discounts.

The closest hotels off the island are at Nyali, the well-to-do suburb immediately to the north of the new Nyali Toll Bridge. Among the best are the Nyali Beach, the Mombasa Beach and the Severin Sea Lodge, described in the next section.

Sport

Most hotels can arrange sailing and big game fishing. Otherwise a place to hire boats is the Bahari Club, near Nyali Bridge (Box 90413, telephone 471316). There is a golf course near the Oceanic Hotel and another in Nyali. The Mombasa showground is also in Nyali, just across the old bridge.

Restaurants and Nightlife

Mombasa has few good restaurants. About the best, both for atmosphere and food, is the Tamarind on the Nyali side of the creek looking towards the old harbour. In the town the Mistral and the Capri have continental cuisine, for Chinese food try the Hongkong and for Italian the Bellavista. The Manor Hotel is reliable, while the grillrooms of the Oceanic, Nyali Beach and Mombasa Beach hotels have a nightclub atmosphere. The International Casino is in the Oceanic. As to nightlife, it's a matter of taking the rough with the smooth. The beach hotels have bands or discos, though the New Florida in Mama Ngina Drive is about the only nightclub *per se*. Or you could spend a sailor's night out at the Sunshine or the Casablanca.

There is one theatre, the Little Theatre Club, on Mnazi Moja Road which provides a good evening's entertainment. Temporary membership is available. There are several cinemas.

The yellow banded taxis are municipally licensed, however always negotiate the price beforehand. Fares in town should be Shs 20/- and to the Nyali area hotels around Shs 70/-. To go further out, say south to Diani Beach would be Shs 400/-.

Reliable car hire firms include United Touring Company, Archers, African Roadways, Avenue Motors, Pollman's and Kenatco Transport. A favourite, and cheap, car to hire is the open mini-moke.

Local tours and game lodge bookings can be made through many agents. Bunson Travel Service Ltd (Box 84965) is deservedly well known. The most popular game viewing tours are to the Tsavo National Park and to the Shimba Hills Reserve, both easily accessible. These are often done by air charter (for firms see Transport and Safaris section). If you want to travel up or down the coast cheaply, do not forget the Mombasa Peugeot Service. A useful map of the city and island is published by Esso.

Mombasa has excellent hospitals, the one most used by Europeans being the privately run Katherine Bibby Hospital, close to the sea. Hotels can provide the names of doctors.

The following countries maintain consuls in the town – Austria, Belgium, Denmark, Finland, France, German Federal Republic, Great Britain, Greece, India, Italy, Netherlands, Norway, Sweden and Switzerland.

North of Mombasa: Beach hotels, Kilifi, Malindi, Lamu

Since the construction of the new Nyali Bridge, traffic normally goes north across it. The toll charge is Shs 1/- for a car. To reach the bridge from the city centre go down Digo Road, continuing into Abdul Nassir Road, then left into Tom Mboya Avenue and it is on the right. It is signed both from the centre and from the Makupa Causeway. Immediately on the other side is a right turn for the showground and the old Nyali route, while the main road continues straight ahead. At this corner the old Freretown bell hangs in a white arch, a reminder of the Church Missionary Society's settlement of freed slaves close by here, whose descendants run their own District Council and keep up their old church. Mombasa was a great centre for 19th century missionary activity and there is a handsome memorial to the German missionary Dr Krapf on English Point. Together with Rebmann, Dr Krapf founded the first Christian Mission in East Africa at Rabai, a few miles inland from Mombasa in the hills, in 1846.

Nyali to Mtwapa Creek

As well as being the most prosperous suburb of Mombasa, Nyali has several of the best beach hotels on the entire coast. They are all signed to the right of the main tarmac road. The best known is the Nyali Beach Hotel (Class A, Box 90581, telephone 471551) which is some six km (four miles) from the bridge. It has recently been completely renovated, has open air dancing and a wide range of evening entertainment. All the major hotels have pools and access to the beach. The Mombasa Beach Hotel (Class B, Box 90414, telephone 471861) is a newer rival, a gleaming white modern block set on a low promontory, with its own shops and entertainment.

Beyond Nyali this immediate stretch of coast is bounded to the north by the Mtwapa Creek 18 km (11 miles) from Mombasa, and there are a host of hotels between Nyali and Mtwapa along the Bamburi, Kenyatta and Shanzu beaches, principally catering for package tours. The Intercontinental Hotel is due to be built at Shanzu. Notable are the Severin Sea Lodge (Class A, Box 82169 Mombasa, telephone 485001) which is in an African architectural style, the rooms being thatched rondavels set among palms trees, and the Serena Beach Hotel at Shanzu, delightfully designed on the lines of the ancient Arab styles of Lamu. The rooms are air conditioned and the food is excellent. The Serena is classed A (bookings Box 48690 Nairobi, telephone 338656). A comfortable less expensive hotel is the Whitesands (Class C, Box 90173 Mombasa, telephone 485926) on Bamburi Beach and the Bamburi Beach Hotel (Class C, Box 83966 Mombasa, telephone 485611) can also be recommended. Unlike some hotels which are overwhelmingly patronised by Germans or Italians, these two keep a balance of nationalities and are popular with English speaking people, as are the Nyali Beach and the Serena. There are also self-help cottages for rent on Bamburi Beach, but not on a centralised basis.

There are number of attractions along this stretch. The Bombolulu Gardens with their jewellery shop near Bamburi are worth a visit and there is an aquarium at Kipepeo. The Sea Haven Restaurant at Shanzu is noted for seafood and the Red Lobster and Le Joli Coin restaurants are pleasant. However the best restaurant here is Le Pichet, just the other side of the toll bridge across Mtwapa Creek. An entertaining nightclub is the Bora Bora on Bamburi beach.

Mtwapa to Kilifi

Mtwapa Creek is quite a centre of activity. Kenya Marineland is there, with a display of some 150 species of tropical fish such as you could see along the reef, including shark and barracuda which are fed daily by a scuba diver. Nearby is a serpentarium with African snakes and crocodiles. F. G. MacConnell and Co organise deep sea fishing, goggling and water-skiing, as do the Adcock Fishing and the Aqua Sports Centre. Le Pichet Restaurant, close to Marineland, is reached by turning right immediately after the bridge. The French style cooking in a large, cool informal dining room is first class. During the day dhow excursions are run from Mombasa to Marineland.

The 40 km (25 mile) length of coral sand between Mtwapa Creek and Kilifi Creek is generally known as 'the north coast' and the main road runs parallel to the shore a short distance inland, with side roads leading to hotels and other sites. While it has long been popular among Kenya residents and there are beach houses to rent, like the Continental Beach Cottages (Box 124 Kikambala), it has not attracted international development and standards are low. At Kanamai there is a youth hostel and camping site run by the National Christian Council of Kenya. In fact the beaches along here are near-perfect and, as everywhere up the coast, water temperatures in the sea range from 78°F to 95°F (27°C to 35°C), hardly less than the average shade temperature on land of 95°F (35°C).

Shortly after the Mtwapa Bridge there is a signed turn-off to the Arab ruins of Jumba la Mtwana, a village dating from about AD 1,350, whose name means 'the large house of the slave'. It was abandoned a century after it was built, for reasons which are as mysterious as they are at the Gedi ruins further north. There are remains of two mosques, the one by the sea being delightfully situated; and evidence of houses and tombs. A guidebook is available and after your tour you can walk on down to the sea and swim. Like other coastal sites, Jumba is a reminder of the many centuries during which the Omani Arabs dominated the coast and there are many such remains all the way up to Lamu. If you are interested, go to the Fort Jesus Museum which has a large scale map, indicating them all, together with photographs. Equally the *Kenya Coast* map, published by the Survey of Kenya, marks them all but without descriptions. They can be overgrown and hard to find.

Here you are in Giriama country and in the villages you will see Giriama women wearing short, white, flouncing skirts, fluffed out by vast bustles of coconut fibre. At Vipingo there are large sisal estates. Incidentally travel up the coast can be cheap, since there are several Peugeot taxi firms which operate like minibuses and charge very reasonably.

Kilifi to Malindi

At Kilifi, 57 km (36 miles) from Mombasa, is the Mnarani Hotel (Class C, Box 81445 Kilifi, telephone 18), a big game fishing establishment with its own airstrip, jetty and facilities for water-skiing, sailing, goggling, scuba diving, and underwater photography, as well as fishing. The hotel is on the south side of Kilifi Creek, which is safe for swimming and which offers one of the most spectacular birdlife sights in Africa. This is the evening flight of hundreds of carmine bee eaters, tiny but splendidly coloured birds who spend the day feeding inland, then return to a small mangrove island just before sunset to roost. You can hire a motorboat from the hotel to watch this and will see herons, egrets and many other waterbirds on the way.

On the other side of the road as you approach the ferry is a path to the Mnarani ruins, mainly distinguished by a fine Arab pillar tomb. The site overlooks the creek. Also on this side is a serpentarium. Crossing the creek involves a toll-free car ferry, but waiting time can vary greatly. If you have a schedule to keep, allow half an hour to get across. The main part of Kilifi, which is basically an administrative centre, is on the north side of the creek, where there is the Seahorse Hotel (Class D, bookings Box 57661 Nairobi, telephone 338599). It is situated on the creek, not on the sea, and the creek's best friends' could hardly claim that the water is clean. The Seahorse caters mainly for German tourists, as does the Mnarani. It has a pool, water-skiing and an agreeable restaurant.

Although there are some excellent and completely deserted beaches beyond Kilifi, further on the access to the sea is less easy and the 61 km (38 miles) of fast road to Malindi passes close to the mangrove swamps of Mida Creek, reaching nothing of much interest until the turn-off to Watamu at Gedi, some 16 km (10 miles) south of Malindi. Here there are the best preserved remains of an Arab town anywhere on the coast, a 15th century settlement which covered 45 acres and only part of which has been recovered from the jungle which rampaged through it until 1948 when it was made a national park and excavations were begun. In the course of the 17th century all the Arab settlements between Somalia and Mtwapa Creek were abandoned as the nomadic Galla tribesmen advanced south. Today you can get a good idea of what it was like in its heyday, with its Great Mosque and fine houses, while the huge trees themselves are fascinating and among the ruins live unique golden rumped elephant shrews. Adjacent to Gedi is the Jilore Forest Reserve, which protects an area of ancient forest and is the home of a great variety of birds.

Watamu
By Gedi is the turn-off to the growing resort of Watamu, which has one of Kenya's few national marine parks, part of a national reserve stretching from Mida Creek up to Malindi. You can swim or water-ski freely, but not collect any seashells. The goggling is superb, especially in the coral garden just inside the reef by Turtle Bay. For this, however, you must pay a park entrance fee of Shs 30/-. Equipment, and glass-bottomed boats can be hired from Ocean Sports Ltd (Box 100 Malindi, telephone Watamu 8) whose shop and informal bar and restaurant are right on the beach. Theirs is some of the best food north of Mombasa, while their rooms, in thatched bandas, are comfortable. The Seafarers Hotel (Box 274, telephone Watamu 6) is next door, while there are two massive package tour hotels in the vicinity, the Turtle Bay Hotel (Box 40503 Nairobi) and the Watamu Beach (Box 300 Malindi). As at Malindi, there are frequent fishing competitions, boats and tackle can be hired and enthusiasts stand with binoculars on the shore identifying the fish recognition pennants that fishermen fly when they have landed a catch. The local colours are yellow for shark, black for tunny, light blue for marlin, green for bonito and white for kingfish or barracuda. Big game fishing is organised here by Mr and Mrs Slater, who have two first class boats and can be contacted through the Ocean Sports. Charges run from Shs 2,600/- a day up to Shs 5000/- for the more luxurious boat, which the novelist Wilbur Smith chartered in the 1983 season.

Near Watamu, within the national reserve, is Mida Creek, one of the best places for bird and marine life on the entire coast. Carmine bee eaters roost here and in March/April and November/December hundreds of species of migrating shore birds pass through. Near the mouth of the creek are Tewa Caves, partly underwater, where giant groupers (up to 800 lbs) and rock cod can be seen close to.

Malindi
Malindi, despite international recognition and recent expansion, is still a delightful small resort with almost everything one could want. There are a few Arab ruins, a single main shopping street, an attractive old town with tall white-washed houses and quiet shadowy byways, and a real beach-combing atmosphere. The bay runs in a wide sweep of sand on to which a break in the reef lets the rollers in (but not the sharks) so it's a good place for surfing. Old timers remember when the beach was much closer to the village, but that was before the sand bar near the mouth of the Sabaki River just north of the town broke, changing the character of the bay and turning the nearer parts of the beach into a brownish coloured sand. However there is no lack of the original beautiful white coral sands out towards Casuarina Point. The other major change is that whereas Malindi used to be rather sleepy, it now offers plenty of hectic evening entertainment.

Historically, Malindi probably dates back to the 9th century. Arabs occupied the site from the 13th century onwards, following Mombasa's example in giving a hostile reception to the Portuguese explorer, Vasco da Gama, although he left a permanent memento of his call in the shape of the white pillar which now stands outside the town on the way to Casuarina Point and is one of the oldest European monuments in Africa. After holding off Turkish and other attacks in the 16th century, Malindi went into decline, following the transfer of the Portuguese headquarters to Mombasa, and the Arabs recovered domination. For nearly three centuries slaves were sold in front of the pillar tombs which stand by the Juma Mosque. The taller of these tombs dates from the 15th century. Malindi's present status began with the building of the first beach hotels in the 1930s, when it started to become popular with British settlers' families, though the tourist boom did not occur until after Independence in the 1960s.

One of the principal events of Malindi's year is the Sea Festival with its fishing contests, held during November, while in February, when the marlin and sailfish are running far out beyond the reef, the International Billfish competition takes place, with participants from all over the world. The hotels can arrange game fishing for you. For goggling and marine life you want to go some four km (three miles) south to Casuarina Point to the Malindi Marine National Park, which has magnificent coral gardens. Normal park entry fees are payable and glass bottomed boats are usually waiting for clients – remember that it's a lot cheaper to go in a group. Also out in this direction is the Birdland Aviary of exotic birds at Silversands and Mark Easterbrook's snake farm, open every day, where you can watch the snakes being fed on Fridays at 16.30. Sports available are golf at the course just north of the town, riding at the Palm Tree Club near the golf course and, of course, windsurfing at any of the hotels, and squash at the Driftwood Club.

Hotels

Malindi has four principal hotels and two hotel/clubs, mainly tied to German and Italian tour operators. The hotels along the main street used to back onto the sea 20 years ago, but the ocean's retreat has left a 200 metre swathe of sand dunes between them and the breakers. The most sophisticated hotel, with English connections, is the Arab style Sindbad (Class C, Box 30 Malindi, telephone 20880). It has an attractive pool. The others, all classified C, are the banda style Lawfords (Box 20 Malindi, telephone 20440) which holds frequent beach barbecues; the Blue Marlin (Box 54 Malindi, telephone 20441) and the Eden Roc (Box 350 Malindi, telephone 20480). These, like the Suli Suli Club (Box 360 Malindi, telephone 317) and the Palm Tree Club (Box 180) out to the north, all have swimming pools and there is a disco at one or the other every night. Three km south of the town, off the road to Casuarina Point, is the completely different Driftwood Club (Box 65 Malindi, telephone 20155) which does not take package tours, has one of the best restaurants in the area, accommodates guests in simple chalets (some air-conditioned) and has its own scuba diving school. Finally, on the road to Casuarina Point, is the Indian Ocean Lodge, an expensive and luxurious establishment, not open to non-residents. The Lodge (bookings Box 171 Malindi, telephone 20394), is a beautiful white Arab style house, situated on a small promontory above a magnificent beach. It has its own pool and gardens and the all-in charge of Shs 2,000/- double a day includes big game fishing and trips to the Galana Lodge described on page 93. At the other extreme, there is a youth hostel and several Shs 20/- a-night-hotels in the old town, such as the New Kenya and New Safari.

Shops selling tourist requisites and banks are along the main street, while the part leading to the old town is lined with souvenir stalls and in the old quarter itself you can get all manner of *kikois, kangas* and beach shorts and dresses made up of local materials. Nafisi's Store is here, about the best shop for high quality curios, genuine Arab silver ornaments and Lamu chests, though there are competitors nearby. For holiday clothes the Rose Boutique, next to the Kenya Airways office, is excellent. The principal tour and travel firms are Bunsons, Pollmans and UTC, and there is an Avis car hire office. In fact, you can manage perfectly well without a car, or if you do want one, rent an open mini-moke, and bicycles are popular. For cheap transport up and down the coast go to the old town where, by asking, you will soon find the MPS office, which runs reliable and clean minibuses and taxis to Mombasa. There is a daily, not so comfortable, bus to Lamu and there are usually several excursion flights a day to Lamu from the airport (Cooper Skybird, telephone 20860). (The Kenya Airways office telephone is 20237 and the airport telephone is 20192.)

Eating out in Malindi is no problem. One of the best restaurants is the Umande, off the road to Casuarina Point, which has French cuisine. It is advisable to book. The Suli Suli Inn serves Italian food and the Palm Garden has Indian dishes. The restaurant at the Driftwood Club has excellent seafood. For nightlife, although all the hotels have discos, the Stardust is outstanding, with lighting effects which would do credit to London or New York.

A variety of excursions are available for the day from Malindi, including the air excursion to Lamu already mentioned. One of the more amusing is the dhow safari on the dhow Tasubiri, which takes people out for a picnic lunch to a secluded beach. Another is to have lunch at Robinson Island, mentioned in a moment, or visit 'Hell's Kitchen' on the Sabaki River. Rather closer, only 13 km (8 miles) to the north is Mambrui, a small fishing village of the Bajun tribe, with an old mosque and its attractive replacement. The other obvious trip is south to see the Gedi ruins and the Marine National Park at Watamu, already described. A longer range safari would be to the Baomo Lodge on the Tana River, described in the Eastern Kenya section. This can be done through Tana River Camp Ltd, in the main street.

Finally, in case of illness, Malindi has several resident doctors and a small hospital (telephone 20490).

Malindi to Garsen and Lamu
The road north from Malindi ceases to be tarmac outside the town and is quite rough. The most distinctive feature of the coastline is the promontory called Ras Ngomeni, further on than Mambrui, which juts out into the Indian Ocean to form one boundary of the huge crescent shaped Ungwana Bay (Formosa Bay). Ras Ngomeni itself offers a paradise of tide-shaped driftwood for beachcombers, while the saltpans between it and the main road are a haunt of waterbirds: you can see pelicans, yellow billed storks, egrets, pied kingfishers and ospreys.

Past Mambrui there are turn-offs the main Garsen road which lead to Che Shale and to Robinson Island, both mini-resorts in their own right, while inland the road along the north bank of the Sabaki River leads to 'Hell's Kitchen'. This is a Grand Canyon in miniature and you reach it by following the road signed to Marafa. By contrast Che Shale is an exclusive, rather sophisticated, beach lodge created by a former hunter, Johnny Aniere and his wife Vanessa. Set among casuarina trees on a long and effectively private beach, it includes full board, wind-surfing and transfers from Malindi in the all-in price, you can go goggling in local coral gardens or go big game fishing. (Bookings either direct to Box 492 Malindi, or through Block Hotels, Box 47557 Nairobi, telephone 335807.) Che Shale is altogether 20 km (12 miles) from Malindi, but the last part needs four-wheel drive. Robinson Island's turn-off is further on, 20 km (12 miles) up the main road. You then drive seven km (four miles) to the shore where there is a car park and a boat to take you across for lunch at a seafood restaurant in a beach banda. The season is August to April and you can book through any local travel agent. Offshore is the launching platform for an Italian/American space rocket programme.

The remainder of the 111 km (69 miles) from Malindi to Garsen has little noteworthy. As mentioned in the Eastern Kenya section Garsen itself is a small town on the Tana River, populated by Somali, Orma and Pokomo people. From here the murram road goes on to Lamu via a ferry, but it can be impassable in the rains. Near Garsen is a heronry, where breeding birds can be seen from May to September. A diversion up-river from Garsen, turning left before the ferry, takes you to Wenje (58 km, 36 miles) and the Tana River Primate Reserve, already described. The principal road, after you have crossed the ferry, continues alongside the Tana River delta and near new settlement schemes until it reaches Mokowe and you take a boat across to Lamu. If you fly into Lamu, the plane lands on Manda island and there are usually boats waiting to ferry you across the creek. Cars are not allowed on Lamu Island.

Lamu

Lamu, together with its sister islands of Manda and Pate, has been inhabited for over a 1,000 years. Each constituted a state, despite the relative smallness of the archipelago, and they dominated each other in turn, engaging in wars which reputedly were interrupted if the tide brought in a big run of fish. Today 65 percent of the people depend on fishing for their livelihood, catching barracuda, kingfish and sea tilapia, though not shellfish. The other principal occupation has always been trade and the dhow trade with Muscat and Saudi Arabia remains more important to Lamu than to any other port on the coast. The picturesque waterfront (shown in the drawing in this section) sees a constant coming and going of boats and there are sometimes great stacks of mangrove poles lying on the quayside awaiting shipment to Arabia. The point about the mangrove is that it grows in swamps by the sea – you pass through mangroves taking the boat from the airfield – and so its wood is impregnated with salt, which deters white ants from eating it. The wood is also hard. For centuries it has been favoured for the construction of houses in Arabia, the length of the average mangrove pole determining the span of ceilings. However Arabian oil wealth has replaced the traditional mangrove poles with steel and concrete and the trade is dying.

Equally the dhows are being replaced by small merchant ships, though dhow building is still important to Lamu. There is a shipyard in the town, with the main one round the other side of the island at Matondoni, and the launching of a new dhow occasions at least two days of celebration. The dhows themselves are made of mahogany. The smaller dhow-like fishing boats – as in the foreground of our illustration – are called *mashuas*. They all have similar triangular sails, but the dhow has a high bow and stern and a deck, as befits a cargo carrier. A large dhow can have a deadweight of 120 tons, carry 400 tons of freight and cost Shs 3,000,000/- to build (approx £150,000). The original Lamu dhow was the *mtepe*, the 'sewn boat', the planks being literally sewn together with cord because the people mistrusted iron nails. You can see a model of one in the museum. Making dhow models is understandably a local speciality.

Overall, Lamu is a unique blend of tradition and informality: the latter making it something of a haven for drop-outs from Europe. Twenty years ago the town had no proper hotel and was 'undiscovered'. Now it has several and tourists on excursions from Mombasa or Malindi may fail to appreciate that beneath the sleepily relaxed exterior, the people are strongly Moslem and proud of their individuality. They do not normally drink and will, for example, be offended if you take alcohol with you for a picnic trip on one of their

Dhows lying off Lamu

boats. The Riyadha Mosque in the town is a centre of learning and in January there is a tremendous celebration for the feast of Maulidi, when thousands of Moslems converge on Lamu and the shops run out of everything. Traditionally three visits to Lamu for Maulidi equal one pilgrimage to Mecca.

Town Tour

If you tour the town you must look out for the museum, which is on the waterfront. Among its prize exhibits are two huge brass and ivory ceremonial horns, or *siwas*. The area between the museum and the fort, an unmistakable castellated structure on a slight hill, is the 17th century town. The fort itself was originally an Omani palace, was fortified by the Portuguese and is now the prison. The narrow streets of the old town have many shops selling carvings. Some of the best buys are brass inlaid chests and silver ornaments. The wood for the traditional Lamu doors comes from the Witu Forest, near the Garsen Road. One good shop to ask for is called Scanda. You should also seek out the makers of model dhows to see their craft, as well as seeing the full scale shipyard. Two books on Lamu are *An Historical Guide to the Lamu Archipelago* by Esmond and Chrysee Martin and *Lamu Town* by James de Vere Allen, who founded the museum.

Hotels

The main hotel in the town is Petley's Inn (Class C, Box 4 Lamu, telephone 48) which is on the waterfront with delightful views from the dining room and has a swimming pool two floors up. The food is good, but the downstairs bar is apt to be noisy. There are a number of cheaper hotels, with no air-conditioning, in the town's back streets – where it can be stifling in hot weather. Probably the best of these is the New Mahrus. The other Class C hotel is in the totally different surroundings of Lamu's other village, Shela, where many miles of superb beach stretch around the point. This hotel is Peponi's (Box 24 Lamu, telephone 29). With a long terrace overlooking the sea, Peponi's is spread out among coconut groves, its accommodation being largely in chalet bedrooms. The food is excellent. Nearby is the old Shela mosque and some very photogenic scenery. You can take a boat from the Lamu waterfront to Shela for about Shs 20/- or walk along the shore, which takes 45 minutes. Across the water, on Manda Island, is the Ras Kitau Beach Hotel (bookable through Flamingo Tours, Box 83321 Mombasa, telephone 311978).

Excursions

The obvious trips from Lamu are all by boat and there is no lack of craft on the waterfront available for hire. One pleasant trip is to go fishing, then sail to a beach on Manda Island where the boatmen cook the fish and you swim until late afternoon. Prices are entirely by negotiation. But be warned; if you decide to go further and sail to Pate – a rewarding visit – remember that you go through the creeks and that *mashuas* require wind to move. We went up to Pate once in three hours – and took seven hours getting back, including being caught on a mudbank when the tide went out.

Pate and Kiwaiyu

Sailing to Pate in the creeks behind Manda Island you pass an attractive private Italian beach club on Manda Bay, where you may be allowed to call in for a drink. Pate itself, like Siyu on the same island, is very run down, but with interesting traces of former glory, such as shards of the Chinese porcelain which once decorated house walls. Gold ornaments are a local speciality. The journey there, past mangrove swamps and creeks alive with birds, makes the trip additionally worthwhile. Oysters from among the mangroves are very tasty.

Beyond Pate is a whole archipelago of coral islands, notably Kiwaiyu Island, of considerable beauty and offering magnificent scuba diving and sailing. They can only be reached effectively by a power boat, or if you are feeling rich, you could hire a floatplane down at Kilifi and fly up for the day. There are two places to stay, both expensive: the Kiwaiyu Island Lodge on the island, and the Kiwaiyu Safari Village on the mainland. You can book through Let's Go Travel (Box 60342 Nairobi, telephone 29539). Prices are around Shs 1,600/- double per day.

South of Mombasa: Diani Beach, Shimoni

The south Kenya coast has deservedly come into its own. The fine white coral beaches here are mostly better than those north of Mombasa and the natural delights are swimming, goggling and big game fishing, though there is less marine life along the reef, not least owing to the depredations of shell and coral souvenir sellers. Although you have to cross Mombasa Harbour on the Likoni ferry, which runs every ten minutes, you are then on a good tarmac road.

Just south of the ferry at Likoni is the enlarged Shelly Beach Hotel (Class D, Box 96030 Mombasa, telephone 45122), a pleasant place to go for a drink or a meal. The reef is more interesting here than further south, though the swimming is not so good. Specimens you may expect to find in the clear greeny-blue water around the reef include brittle stars, a kind of starfish whose arms break off but grow again, and a variety of conch shells, among them the rare foot-long giant spider conch. Along Shelly Beach there are also a children's resort centre and a camping site.

Shimba Hills National Reserve

Between the village of Waa and Tiwi a road branches off inland to the village of Kwale and the Shimba Hills Reserve, known for its handsome sable antelope. The main gate is 17 km (10½ miles) from the turn-off and takes half an hour, going through the village of Kwale, where you are 1,200 ft above sea level. It's better not to take the earlier entrance, before Kwale, as it does not lead into the main circuits of the reserve, which are well sign-posted. The area is largely thick forest, inhabited by many animals including the small forest elephant. However we only saw herds out on the Lango Plains near Giriama Point, where the trees give way to rolling parkland along an escarpment. This is one of the few reserves where you are allowed out of your car, but forest elephant have a reputation for ill temper, so keep your distance. Camping sites are available (ask at the gate) but there is no lodge. All the beach hotels arrange day tours.

Along Tiwi Beach, as further down the coast, there are beach cottages to rent at anything from Shs 200/- a day for two bedrooms in simple style, to Shs 800/- for luxury with servants included. There is no one agent, so the best plan is to book through one of the major Nairobi tour operators, such as UTC.

Tiwi Beach is separated from the celebrated Diani Beach by the estuary of the Mwachema River. On the south side, close to the sea, is a well preserved ancient Persian mosque in a grove of giant baobab trees. Persian, Arab and Portuguese ships all used the estuary for shelter if they could not reach Mombasa. A word of warning, however, do not walk here or anywhere away from the hotels either alone or carrying valuables. There have been many robberies.

Diani Beach

The five km (three mile) stretch of white coral sand fringed by palm trees known as Diani Beach has seen more recent development than any other part of the coast. It has an airfield at Ukunda and there is a small shopping complex with a supermarket, bank, boutiques and amusement centre. Altogether there are ten hotels along the beach, which has a tarmac access road signed from the main coast road just before Ukunda. Among the longer established hotels which are favourites of English visitors are the Trade Winds (Class C, Box 8 Ukunda, telephone Diani Beach 2016), which has been expanded but retains its comfortable informality and the Two Fishes (class B, Address P O Ukunda, telephone Diani Beach 2101). They both belong to African Tours and Hotels and can be booked in Nairobi (Box 30471, telephone 336858). Another family hotel is the Jadini, greatly improved to a Class A standard (Box 84616 Mombasa, telephone Diani Beach 2051). The most luxurious hotel is the Diani Reef (Class A, Box 35 Ukunda, telephone Diani Beach 2175). Like most of the others it has all the facilities you would expect in a Mediterranean resort hotel, as have the Leopard Beach (Class A, Box 34 Ukunda, telephone Diani Beach 2111). and the Africana Sea Lodge (Class A, Box 84616 Mombasa, telephone Diani Beach 2136).

Not all hotels particularly encourage outside visitors to use their facilities. The Robinson's Baobab, for all its English name, is effectively a German club. All the hotels have pools, discos, tour operators' offices, shops and busy programmes of entertainments and watersports, but none – except perhaps the Diani Reef and the Leisure Lodge – is significantly different to any luxury package tour beach hotel anywhere else in the world. If you do not want to stay in a hotel at all, then there are quite a number of good villas and beach cottages to rent through Wailes Agency, whose office is near the Leopard Beach Hotel. There is also one luxury safari camp, run by Nomad Safaris (PO Ukunda, telephone Diani Beach 2155) which is well situated by the beach and has a first class restaurant. All the hotels organise excursions to Mombasa, the average bus fare being Shs 75/-. There is a diving school at the Jadini Hotel.

Big Game Fishing

However the real sea attractions down here are out in the Indian Ocean, where black and striped marlin, sailfish, barracuda, shark, tunny, five-fingered jack, kingfish, wahoo and bonito cruise in the almost unexploited deep water beyond the reef. The main Diani fishing expert, with several boats and full tackle, is John Bland (Box 47 Ukunda, telephone Diani Beach 2087), who operates from the Jadini Hotel. Other boats are run by Nomad Safaris, (telephone Diani Beach 2156 for boats). Costs are around Shs 300/- per hour per boat. Count on at least four hours. John Bland also hires out diving equipment and has a glass bottomed boat for viewing the reef.

Apart from the Shimba Hills National Reserve, there are relatively few inland attractions near Diani, and many holidaymakers take flying safaris to the Mara or to Tsavo. However you should look out for an extraordinary baobab tree near the Trade Winds Hotel. Baobabs are said, in local legend, to have been pulled up and re-planted upside down by the devil, which is why the branches look like roots. This one is estimated to be 500 years old and has a girth of 21.69 metres (71 ft 2 ins). This giant specimen of a tree you often see in the coastal region is protected. Cashew nut trees are also common down here while in the nearby Jadini Forest you will find innumerable butterflies, birds and monkeys. Look out specially for the black and white colobus monkey, with long white hair round its head and shoulders.

Diani to Shimoni
To continue down the coast you must return to the main tarmac road at Ukunda. Pending any new developments, held up at the time of writing by the world recession, there is little noteworthy except fine beaches near Gazi and Funzi. At a location called Four Twenty South there are beach cottages which can be rented through Mr Martin (Box 30583 Nairobi, telephone 60960). Then, some 80 km (50 miles) from Mombasa, you reach the village of Ramisi and the sign to the world famous Pemba Channel Fishing Club (Box 54 Ukunda, telephone Msambweni 5Y2). The last 16 km (10 miles) from Ramisi is rough going, but that will hardly deter enthusiasts, because the Pemba Channel offers some of the finest fishing in Africa and many records have been established here, especially for marlin and shark. Furthermore the Manager, Mr Pat Hempill, lets you keep the catch or else will sell it for you and credit your account. This is not usually possible elsewhere. The rooms are chalets with bath or shower. Full board is Shs 200/- per day.

Kisiti National Marine Park
From Shimoni you can also take a boat to snorkel in the Kisiti National Marine Park, which encompasses four reef islets and their coral gardens. Wasini Island, just offshore, has a restaurant with a good reputation for its seafood. A dhow makes the short trip across for lunch.

South of Shimoni is the Tanzania border, closed at the time of writing. If you were to cross, you would continue on the main tarmac road from Ramisi and eventually get to Tanga.

Lions taking their siesta near Lake Manyara

Northern Tanzania

The Country

The highest, the longest, the deepest, the most vast, the most numerous – all these adjectives can be applied to the many attractions which Tanzania offers to the visitor. The first recorded mention of it occurs in the *Periplus of the Erythraean Sea*, a detailed mariner's guide to the East African coast dating from the first century AD. This document refers to the island of Menouthias, probably Zanzibar or Pemba, and the mainland town of Rhapta, possibly Pangani or another town in the Rufiji River delta.

A number of settlements were made on the coast by Arabs and possibly Persians, the most famous and best preserved being Kilwa in the south. Bagamoyo, a small town just north of Dar es Salaam, was the favourite jumping-off spot for the 19th century explorers, including Livingstone, Stanley, Burton and Speke, as well as being the start and end of the great slave caravans from the interior.

As Tanganyika, the country became a sovereign state on December 9, 1961. Previously it had been a German colony from the 1880s until 1916, and after that a United Nations Trusteeship administered by Britain. It became a republic within the Commonwealth exactly a year after *Uhuru* (Swahili for independence), under the Presidency of Dr Julius Nyerere, who was the country's first Prime Minister. Then on April 27, 1964, a union was formed between Tanganyika and the islands of Zanzibar and Pemba, taking the name of the 'United Republic of Tanzania'. Mwalimu Dr Nyerere became President of this new state. A new capital city is currently being laid out at Dodoma, for completion in the late 1980s, but Dar es Salaam will remain the commercial centre.

Today the country's 937,062 sq km are the home of over 120 different tribes, the largest being the Sukuma. The total population is 18 million, including a small percentage of Arabs, Asians and Europeans.

Within Tanzania's borders lie Africa's highest mountain, Kilimanjaro; its deepest and longest freshwater lake, Tanganyika; and the largest game reserve in the world, the 16,000 square mile Selous; as well as the finest concentration of wildlife in the world on the Serengeti Plains. Overall, both the most spectacular and the most accessible areas lie in Northern Tanzania, on which this chapter concentrates. However, Dar es Salaam is still the main point of entry to Tanzania, especially for business visitors.

The north has often been described as a microcosm not just of Tanzania but of East Africa as a whole. Its scenery ranges from the vast, golden plains of the Serengeti to the snowcapped peaks of Mount Kilimanjaro, from wild bush country to neatly tended farms and plantations, from tumbling mountain streams to lakes pink from the flamingoes flocking round them, over rolling grasslands and through tropical rainforests. Among the people are prosperous African farmers, operating highly mechanised farms, peasant cultivators still using the primitive digging stick and pastoral nomads like the famous warrior tribe, the Masai.

The main attraction is, of course, the unsurpassed concentration of wildlife, the greatest in Africa. Almost wherever you go, even on the main highways, you can generally expect to see zebra, wildebeest, ostrich and antelope. In fact, one of the most frequent road signs on the Arusha-Moshi road is 'Danger – game area', illustrated by a leaping buck. Furthermore, visits to the incomparable Serengeti Plains, Kilimanjaro, Lake Manyara and the Ngorongoro and Ngurdoto Craters can be made without strain in a short tour, since they are not far apart and the roads are reasonable, except during the rains.

The Kilimanjaro International Airport at Sanja Juu, 56 km (35 miles) from Arusha, means that visitors can fly straight from overseas into the heart of Tanzania's safari country.

Climate

Northern Tanzania is a semi-temperate region with two rainy seasons a year, the long rains in April and May and the short rains in either October or November. This means that the best seasons for safaris are July to October and December to February. Mean temperatures vary between 62°F and 85°F (17°C and 30°C) and there is frost and snow on high ground. The nights are cool. In the evenings, especially from June to October and during the rainy seasons, warm clothing is necessary. There is low humidity and the area is virtually free from mosquitoes, though mosquito nets are provided in some hotels.

Hotels and Game Lodges

A chain of hotels and game lodges is run by the Tanzania Tourist Corporation, who run a centralised booking system through their Dar es Salaam office (Box 2485, telephone 27671/4, telex 41061). These hotels are indicated by (TTC) in the text. They maintain good standards. Prices at the time of writing (1983) ranged from Shs 460/- for a single room with bed and breakfast to Shs 600/- for a double room. Lodges normally offer full board. There are special cheap low season rates at the lodges (and beach hotels) from April 15 to June 30. A hotel levy of 12½ percent is included in these prices.

Other hotels, especially in provincial towns, often charge less and it is often possible to stay a night for Shs 100/- or so. Addresses for booking non-TTC hotels are given in the text, but no prices since these are so subject to change.

The cost of meals varies widely. Outside Dar es Salaam and Arusha, menus are likely to be simple, except of course in the game lodges. A snack will cost up to Shs 40/-, while a full meal in a good restaurant will be Shs 100/- or more. Beer costs Shs 22/- a bottle and soft drinks almost as much. Tanzania has also started making her own Dodoma rosé and red wine.

National Parks and Reserves

President Nyerere's Arusha Manifesto of 1967 was a landmark in African game conservation, 'Wildlife is an integral part of our resources', he said. Today 25 percent of the country's area is devoted to parks and reserves. The famous ones in the north are:

Arusha National Park
116 sq km (45 sq miles). Combines three formerly independent sanctuaries – the 1½-mile-wide Ngurdoto Crater, the Mount Meru Crater, and the Momella lakes, scene of many films. Elephant, rhino buffalo and smaller game. Open all the year. See page 120.

Lake Manyara National Park
318 sq km (123 sq miles) in the Rift Valley south west of Arusha. Noted for its 340 species of birds and for the lions that take their siestas in its trees. Open all the year. See page 123.

The Ngorongoro Crater
The floor area of this fantasic 2,000 ft deep volcanic crater is 113 sq km. It is the centre of a 8,290 sq km (3,200 sq mile) conservation area which is a pioneer experiment in reconciling the interests of wildlife and forests with the needs of the local Masai tribe. Large herds of plains game. See page 124.

The Serengeti National Park
About 14,760 sq km (5,700 sq miles) between Arusha and Lake Victoria, it contains the most spectacular concentration of plains game anywhere in the world. Open all the year. Lodges. See also page 125.

Entry fees to the national Parks are between Shs 20/- and Shs 40/- per adult per day for non-residents. Ranger guides are well worth hiring. In Tanzania's parks and game reserves hunting is permitted from July to December under the control of the Tanzania Wildlife Corporation (Box 114, Arusha), a Government-sponsored organisation which has been introducing special types of cheaper hunting safaris as well as photographic and game viewing tours.

No special permission is required to travel in the game reserves which are administered by the Game Division of the Ministry of Natural Resources and Tourism. The entry fee is Shs 40/- per 24 hours and ranger guides can be hired for Shs 30/- a day. The use of campsites in the parks and reserves costs Shs 40/- per night.

Transport and Safaris

In addition to the scheduled services of Air Tanzania Corporation, the airline offers air charter, as do Tanzania Aviation Ltd, Tanzanair and Flight Service International, all based at Dar es Salaam.

Car hire is available in large towns, but seldom on a self-drive basis. However, the cost of the driver is modest. Typical standing charges are Shs 300/- a day plus Shs 7/50- per kilometre.

Extensive, cheap local bus services operate, but they are usually crowded.

Trains run on both the original railways system linking Dar es Salaam with Arusha, Mwanza and Kigoma, and the intermediate towns, while the Tazara Railway from Dar to Zambia passes through Mbeya. Train tickets are cheap.

While there are private safari firms and tour operators listed in the text, the major firms are the government owned State Travel Service (Head Office, Box 1369, Arusha), represented overseas by TTC, and Bushtrekker Safaris (Box 88, Arusha and Box 5350, Dar es Salaam). Hunting is organised by the Wildlife Corporation and its subsidiaries. For information on any of these consult the TTC which has offices in London (43 Hertford Street, London W1Y 7TF); New York (201 East 42 Street, New York 10017: 8th floor); and in Frankfurt, Milan and Stockholm. The Head Office is in Dar es Salaam (Box 2485, telephone 27671) and the Arusha telephone number is 3152.

Moshi, Mount Kilimanjaro, Arusha

Driving from Kilimanjaro Airport, which is where most people will arrive, you fork left for Arusha and right for Moshi, while Kilimanjaro rises – probably into cloud – on your right and Mount Meru is to the left.

Moshi is the principal centre of the Tanzanian coffee industry, and buyers from all parts of the world attend the coffee auctions there. It is also the administrative headquarters of the Kilimanjaro region, with almost one million people, mostly from the Chagga tribe, who run notable coffee-growing cooperatives. The Chagga are known for the beauty of their women. In fact they live at one end of what has often been described as Tanzania's 'belt of beauty' stretching from the Chagga of Kilimanjaro to the Wabondei of Tanga, with the Wapere of Pare in between. The town is slightly larger than Arusha and is connected with Nairobi by rail (the line does not operate at present), while a branch runs from it to Arusha. Fine views of the snows of Kilimanjaro can be had from the Moshi Hotel, a large, airy hotel, run by the TTC. Other, cheaper, places to stay are the Coffee Tree Hostelry and the Waremi Hotel, while the YMCA on the Moshi-Arusha road is very active. It has a swimming pool, tennis, and organises mountain climbs.

Land Rovers, minibuses and cars can be hired through the State Travel Service office in the Moshi Hotel. Reliable taxi services are operated by Aziz Taxis and Kilimanjaro Tourist Cabs. Air charters can be arranged through the travel agents, Emslies Ltd (telephone Moshi 2071). There are daily scheduled flights to Dar es Salaam by Air Tanzania.

The Moshi Club has an excellent golf course facing Mount Kilimanjaro, and there are tennis courts at the Gymkhana Club.

Mount Kilimanjaro

The 19,340-ft Kibo Peak of Mount Kilimanjaro dominates Moshi, where daily life is closely linked with the mountain. Climbing expeditions start from the town, and many people are drawn here by the magnificence and mystery of this, the highest mountain in Africa, lying only three degrees south of the Equator yet crowned with a permanent icecap. Often the only visible sign of the mountain is the great, snow-mantled shoulder of Kibo (19,340 ft) and the rugged crags of Mawenzi (16,890 ft) thrusting through a ring of cloud. The lower slopes and forests are hidden.

The roof of Africa ranks among the highest volcanic mountains of the world, consisting of three separate volcanoes of different ages which have been welded into one great mass covering an area of 89 km by 61 km (56 miles by 38 miles). The oldest of these volcanoes, known as Shira (13,140 ft), is 12 km (7½ miles) to the west of Kibo, while Mawenzi is 28 km (17½ miles) to the east. Kibo is the youngest of the volcanoes.

The first European to see Kibo was Johannes Rebmann in 1848 and the first to reach its highest point was Hans Meyer, in 1892. Climbers traditionally follow the route taken by most of the early explorers. They start from Marangu – which means 'many waters' – where the Kibo Hotel (Box 102, Moshi) and Marangu Hotel (Box 40, Moshi) are situated, 5,000 ft up and 40 km (25 miles) from Moshi. Neither hotel is expensive.

Around the hotels there are plantations of coffee, maize and bananas. From here, climbers pass through the forest belt which ends at 10,000 ft. The first night stop is made at Mandara Hut (9,000 ft). Then they emerge on to the grasslands, near a volcanic cone known locally as *Kimangi Marangu* – 'the small chief of Marangu' – which until not long ago was the site for rain-making ceremonies.

The second stop is made at Horombo Hut (12,300 ft), near the start of the moorlands, glaciers and snow. Dotted around are giant lobelia and groundsel. On the third day, climbers reach Kibo Hut, 3,000 ft below the summit. The final ascent usually begins about 03.00 so that Gillmans Point (18,635 ft) can be reached by about dawn, when there is a good chance of a clear view of the plains below and of the glorious sunrise behind Mawenzi.

One of the main attractions of the ascent of Kilimanjaro is that it does not require mountaineering experience, nor is any special climbing equipment needed for Kibo if the normal route is followed. The climb can be done by any normally healthy person, though considerable physical endurance is required over the five days needed to make the ascent.

New routes up have also been developed. For instance one can drive up to 15,000 ft on the Shira plateau, seeing the game in the national park, then climb this 'plateau route'.

Mawenzi, however, should only be attempted by experienced mountaineers, using normal Alpine climbing gear. Advice for those wishing to attempt this climb can be obtained from the Kilimanjaro Mountain Club (Box 66, Moshi), the TTC, or the Director of National Parks (Box 3134, Arusha). The TTC can provide a route map for climbers.

The mountain can be climbed in almost any month except during the long rains in April and May, but the best months are January, February, September and October, when there are very often cloudless days.

Both the Kibo and Marangu hotels have been arranging safaris for more than 30 years. Costs are reasonable, with reductions for large parties. This includes everything from guides downwards; though clothing, which the hotels can provide, is extra. The guides – absolutely essential for any safari – and porters are very experienced, many having made more than 100 ascents each.

Many places of interest can be visited from Marangu, such as the Ura River with its spectacular waterfalls and the Msumbe Spring, said to have been the home of a snail endowed with powers to revive warriors killed in battle. There are fine walks and visitors often find themselves being accompanied by friendly Chagga children, who like to invite their newfound friends into their homes.

Fishermen can find plenty of sport in the mountain streams and trout rods can be hired from either of the hotels.

Kilimanjaro, 'the shining mountain', has its legends, like all other mountains. *Kibo,* pronounced by the old people 'kiboo' as an exclamation of wonder, has a cave at its foot known as *Nyumba ya Mungu* – 'The House of God'.

The ancient stones of Umbo, situated at Machame and Uru, pillars about six ft above ground level and rammed deeply into the earth, are said to have been places of initiation. The story is told at Uru that they were put in by white people with broad shoulders who reached Kilimanjaro from the west in great numbers, searching for cedarwood and ivory with which to build and decorate the palace of their King, Semira. The story goes that they found cedar at Nanjara in Usseri near the eastern part of Kilimanjaro and that the King was actually Solomon and his palace the temple at Jerusalem.

Kilimanjaro National Park

A wide variety of animal life, including elephant, buffalo, rhino, eland, colobus and blue monkeys, and the rare Harvey's and Abbott's duiker can be seen in the 1,665 sq km (643 sq mile) Kilimanjaro National Park, which includes rainforest, moorland, tundra and the extraordinary giant plant growths that characterise the East African mountains. For more information about the Alpine flora see the description of Mount Kenya on page 74. Like the Arusha National Park, this park also protects vegetation and is used for research. Elephant have been seen at 16,000 ft, and the skeleton of a leopard found above the snowline, where there are known to be wild dogs too.

Arusha National Park and Ngurdoto Crater

The tarmac road from Moshi to Arusha stretches across the Sanya Plains, and several species of game are usually seen on the drive between the towns. About 21 km (13 miles) from Arusha is the turn-off for the 116 sq km (45 mile) Arusha National Park, which includes the Momella Lakes, the Ngurdoto Crater, and the former Mount Meru Crater National Park.

The great attraction of the Arusha National Park is that within its small area it contains such a variety of scenery, including lakes and the ancient forest on Mount Meru's slopes. The park is only 50 km (31 miles) from Arusha, can easily be visited inside a day, and is open throughout the year. The best months to see it are from July to March.

Momella was formerly a game farm run from 1907 by the Trappe family. The remarkable Mrs Trappe was the first woman to become a professional hunter in East Africa and her grandson, Adolf, is now a hunter in Tanzania. She made Momella into a sanctuary in German times and it became a National Park in 1960. It is a most beautiful area that includes five large lakes, tranquil and untypical of Africa, with a tremendous amount of birdlife and a heavy concentration of wildlife, including elephant, buffalo, rhino, giraffe, waterbuck, bushbuck, hippo and colobus monkey. It lies in a saddle between Mount Meru in the west and Kilimanjaro in the east and is spectacularly lovely on a clear day when the mountains can be seen high in the sky. The Mount Meru Crater, an extinct volcano like Kilimanjaro, and its splendid surroundings is one of the best places to see Colobus monkeys. Camping is permitted on Mount Meru at Shs 40/- per night and you can book through the Park Warden (Box 3134, Arusha) or the State Travel Service. There is also a campsite near the Ngurdoto gate.

Ngurdoto is a beautiful miniature crater about one and a half miles across and a few hundred feet deep. A ring road gives access to several vantage points on the crater rim but visitors are not allowed into the crater itself. The crater walls are heavily forested and on the well-watered floor almost every type of animal can be seen while the visitor picnics in glades on the wooded rim. It was described by Sir Julian Huxley, the naturalist, as 'a gem of a park'.

One curiosity of the area is that the only resident predators are leopards. Lions come in, but never stay, having been effectively eliminated by the early farmers and hunters.

The Arusha National Park is served by a rustic hotel called the Momella Lodge, at Usa River, on the edge of the park. Originally constructed as a film set, the lodge has since been rebuilt and is an ideal place for someone who does not want the strain of a strictly scheduled tour, but prefers to have a base from which to make sorties into the surrounding country as the mood takes him. However, the road is rough and four-wheel drive is recommended. Rates for a double room are Shs 440/- bed and breakfast.

In the same area, approximately 20 km (12 miles) from Arusha, off the Arusha to Moshi road, is the Mount Meru Game Sanctuary, where the Hungarian-born Dr von Nagy welcomes visitors to look around his natural zoo, open from 10.30 to 19.00. The Game Sanctuary shelters leopard, elephant, warthog, buffalo and buck, among other species. The Lodge (Box 659 Arusha, telephone Usa River 43), also convenient for the Arusha National Park, is clean, comfortable and strongly recommended.

As you approach Arusha, the scenery becomes more and more tropical, with banana plantations along the road, and the thickly forested slopes of Mount Meru beyond. Thirteen km (8 miles) from Arusha there is a turn off for Lake Duluti, a very pretty and fairly deep crater lake, where you can swim and fish for tilapia. Numerous waterbirds can be seen along the lakeshore and among the reeds.

Arusha

Arusha is an old trading post that is now the most important town in Northern Tanzania, the administrative headquarters of its region, and the place where President Nyerere set out the famous 'Arusha Manifesto' on game preservation. Its position on the Great North Road, halfway between Cairo and the Cape, is marked by a plaque near the New Arusha Hotel, and it is also the exact geographical centre of East Africa.

Despite its recent rapid growth, Arusha has managed to retain a pioneering air, yet in places is paradoxically reminiscent of an English town. Behind it tower the slopes of Mount Meru. Its avenues are riotous with Nandi flame trees and blue-flowering jacarandas, while brightly dressed Africans walk proudly through the busy streets, gathering in the markets, where they will usually consent to be photographed – for a small fee.

There are modern shops in the northern part of the town and in the Arusha International Conference Centre, but it is also worth visiting the bustling, colourful bazaar. Among the best local buys are wood carvings by the famous Makonde tribe of southern Tanzania; skin articles like wallets and handbags, meerschaum pipes, which are made locally; and various semi-precious stones mined in the country, notably rubies, sapphires, zircons, moonstones, tourmalines, garnets and tanzanite, a beautiful blue semi-precious stone. The town has chemists, outfitters and other shops concerned with the safari business, though stocks of European products are limited and prices high. The national Bank of Commerce has branches in Uhuru Road and Clock Tower Square. There is a ladies hairdresser in the New Arusha Hotel. On Sundays services are held at a number of churches and if you are ill there is the small Mount Meru Hospital.

Tour operators include the State Travel Service (Box 1369, telephone 3300, 3113), Subzali Tours and Safaris (Box 3061) and Emslies (Box 24). All these can arrange car hire. George Dove Safaris (Box 1182) operates in conjunction with the Tarangire Tented Camp (see below). For official travel information consult the State Travel Service. Taxis are available in the town.

Arusha has a number of hotels. One of the best is the spacious Mount Meru Hotel (TTC), set in beautiful grounds about a kilometre from the centre of the town, overlooking the slopes of the mountain. It has a swimming pool and is adjacent to a golf course. The restaurant is one of the best places to eat in Arusha. The Hotel Seventy Seven (TTC), also slightly out of town, is constructed like a village, with tennis, swimming and golf, while the New Arusha Hotel (Box 88, telephone 3241) also has a pool and gardens stretching down to the river. The less expensive New Safari Hotel (TTC) is famous. In the bar innumerable photographs of game, leopard skins, Masai shields and spears, and the long, shining copper bar top, create an atmosphere well known to Ernest Hemingway on his visits. The hotel was extended and modernised in 1978. Other places to stay include the Hotel Equator (adjacent to the New Arusha and under the same management), the attractively positioned Tanzanite Hotel (Box 3063, telephone Usa River 32) six miles out on the Moshi road, and the YMCA, which is behind the New Safari Hotel.

Local sports include fishing for trout in the Temi River for which a licence has to be obtained from the New Arusha Hotel. There is a 9-hole golf course at the Gymkhana Club. Mountaineering enthusiasts can tackle Mount Meru (14,978 ft) in a day, starting from an advanced point reached by car, or they can do it at a more leisurely pace, taking three days. The climb is little more than a stiff scramble. Legend has it that Mount Meru was once higher than Kilimanjaro, but volcanic activity made it subside. On a clear day you can see that it has a lesser peak. The two are known locally as 'Big Meru' and 'Little Meru'.

Arusha is a major starting point for hunting and photographic safaris. In fact, 21 of the 29 species of game which may be shot by the holder of a general game licence are to be found in Northern Tanzania, while some of the rarer species are more easily obtained here than anywhere else in East Africa, especially the greater kudu and the sable antelope. The hunting season is from July to December. Complete hunting or photographic safaris are organised by Tanzania Wildlife Corporation (Box 1144, Arusha) who handle taxidermy and the shipping of trophies. For prices write to them. See also the section on Hunting and Photographic Safaris on page 33.

The main northern Tanzania safari circuit runs westwards past Lake Manyara and the Ngorongoro Crater to the Serengeti Plains, while the road going north leads to the Kenya border, closed to tourists at the time of writing.

Lake Manyara, Tarangire, the Ngorongoro Crater

For the first 75 km (46 miles) towards Manyara you are on a tarmac road, but after the turn off to the right at Makuyuni you come on to a murram surface and the going is much rougher from here on right through to the Serengeti. The one entrance to the Lake Manyara National Park is 50 km (31 miles) from the turn-off.

This 318 sq km (123 sq mile) park was originally one of the most popular hunting grounds in East Africa because of the profusion of wildlife, and the protection afforded by its present status has resulted in a spectacular concentration of animals for such a small area. As its name makes clear, the Park is around the lake, which lies at the foot of a dramatic escarpment and only a third of the area of the Park is dry land. Nonetheless it includes five distinct vegetation areas – from forest with high mahogany trees, through light woodland, scrub and open plains to marshland. If you make an early start, and hire a ranger guide, you should easily see three of the 'Big Five' game animals in a day, though in wet conditions you will need a four-wheel drive vehicle to get down the escarpment.

The lions in Manyara have the habit of spending most of the day spread out along the branches of acacia trees, as is shown in the illustration at the start of this chapter, presumably because it is cooler ten or 20 ft up than on the ground. The Park is also famous for its elephant, which now number around 450 – the highest density of elephant population in Africa. They particularly like the sparse woodland by the escarpment, which is where the naturalist Ian Douglas-Hamilton and his wife Oria gained the experiences for their book *Among the Elephants*. Manyara is also an excellent place to see hippo. Since the level of the lake began to fall in 1978, thus increasing the salinity of the remaining water, the hippo have moved to find fresher water and now congregate where the Simba River flows into the lake. They number at least 200.

Manyara is as famous for its birds as its animals, and a small hide has been built on the edge of the soda lake for the use of enthusiastic birdwatchers. At certain times of the year, thousands of flamingoes form a solid line of shimmering pink, stretching many miles down the lake while among the 340 species are duck, waders, jacanas, egrets, ibises and storks. In the acacia woodlands and along the open grasslands are kingfishers, plovers, coursers, larks and wagtails.

The Lake Manyara Hotel (TTC) is perched on the edge of the Rift Wall with a magnificent view overlooking the park, and rhino, buffalo, elephant and other animals can be seen from the hotel grounds. There is a swimming pool, gift shop and beauty salon. Land Rovers and mini-buses can be hired and guides are available at the park gate. There are also campsites which can be booked through the Park Warden and a hostel at the gate.

From Lake Manyara you can either return to the main road and head south or continue westwards to Ngorongoro and Serengeti. The first route which leads to Dodoma and Southern Tanzania brings you to the Tarangire National Park, an area of more than 700 sq miles, designated as a park particularly to protect rhino, oryx and lesser kudu.

Tarangire National Park

The Tarangire National Park lies due south of Lake Manyara and its entrance gate is 107 km (67 miles) from Arusha, four km from the tarmac road. It is the only place in Tanzania where you can view fringe-eared oryx easily and during the dry season the river attracts large concentrations of ungulates – whereas in the Serengeti wildebeest, zebra and others are more dispersed. Other big game are plentiful and include elephant, buffalo, lion and greater kudu. 10 km (6 miles) from the gate there is a tented camp, bookings through Tarangire Tented Camp (Box 1182 Arusha, telephone 3265). There is an airstrip and a petrol station – though as elsewhere petrol may be in short supply.

This part of Tanzania is noted for neolithic graves and rock paintings. Some of the best and most accessible paintings are at Kolo at the foot of the Rift Wall. Kolo is 249 km (156 miles) south of Arusha on the Great North Road. Visitors must be accompanied by one of the government guides who are there. There are 11 protected sites in the area, out of more than a 1,000, many not yet fully examined.

The paintings, associated with various Stone Age cultures, are usually dark red and depict animals, hunting scenes and various symbols. At least a dozen styles are discernible and the earliest work is perhaps 3,000 years old, the newest only 200. But no one knows for sure who did the paintings. A good selection can be seen in a day before driving on to Dodoma.

Returning to the Lake Manyara area, the road to the world-famous Serengeti Plains winds up through spectacular scenery towards the Ngorongoro Crater. On the way, near Karatu some 25 km (16 miles) from Manyara, is Gibb's Farm, a pleasant guest house in what was originally a German settler's house. This is a good alternative to the lodges as a base for visiting the area. The owners can arrange transport, offer home cooking and take only a limited number of guests. Write to Mrs Margaret Gibb. (Gibb's Farm, Box 1501, Karatu). From Karatu it is 40 km (25 miles) to the Ngorongoro Crater. Driving direct from Arusha takes about four hours.

The Ngorongoro Crater

This unique volcanic crater is the heart of a 8,290 sq km (3,200 sq mile) conservation area that contains the greatest permanent concentration of wildlife in Africa in a setting of unequalled grandeur. Some 10,000 Masai live near Ngorongoro with their 100,000 cattle, sharing the land with the wildlife. The fantastic crater itself, a *caldera* or 'collapsed' volcano, is 2,000 ft deep and its flattish floor is 18 km (10 miles) wide. You need four-wheel drive to go down into it, but once there you find one of the wonders of Africa, where approximately 14,000 wildebeest, 5,000 zebra and hundreds of gazelle graze, while the Ngorongoro lions are almost as famous as those of the neighbouring Serengeti. With luck an early morning visitor will see at least one lion and his mate tearing at a kill of wildebeest or zebra, with the attendant scavengers, hyena, jackal and vultures hovering nearby. The State Travel Service operates Land Rovers into the crater, charging Shs 750/- for a half day or Shs 1000/- for a full day. Consult them or the Conservator about taking your own vehicle down, and about camping. There are several camping sites in the crater and they can also be booked through the Ngorongoro Conservation Authority office in Arusha (Box 776).

However most people will stay at one or other of the lodges, perhaps the best being the Ngorongoro Crater Lodge, which is perched on the lip of the crater. It has a log cabin style dining room, lounge and bar. Most other buildings are of log construction, their rural aspect contrasting strongly with the high standard of comfort inside. Warm clothing is advisable for early mornings and evenings as the lodge is nearly 8,000 ft above sea level. (Bookings: Box 751 Arusha, telephone 3530.) Another place to stay is the comfortable Ngorongoro Wildlife Lodge (TTC), similarly overlooking the crater. More simple accommodation is available at the Ngorongoro Rhino Lodge (Box 445, Arusha) which is owned by the Conservation Authority.

Olduvai Gorge, the Serengeti, Mwanza

From Ngorongoro it is well worth stopping at the Olduvai Gorge en route to the Serengeti, which is 57 km (36 miles) along the gravelled, but rough, road.

Olduvai has been called the cradle of mankind. Here very early human remains, 1¾ million years old, forming what has become known as the Nutcracker Man, were found by Dr L. S. B. Leakey. The skull of *Zinjanthropus boisei*, to give it its scientific name, is now in the National Museum in Dar es Salaam. In late 1963, Dr Leakey and others found remains which are believed to be even older than the Nutcracker Man. Fossils were first seen here by a German butterfly collector in 1911. There is a small museum where guides and publications are available. Many of the other finds from Olduvai are also in the National Museum.

The Serengeti National Park

At Olduvai you are close to the boundary of the Serengeti, one of the finest game areas in the world.

The Serengeti National Park encompasses the largest migratory concentration of plains game to be found anywhere in the world. The northern boundary adjoins the famed Mara game country of Kenya, while to the west the Park stretches in a long 'corridor' to within two miles of Lake Victoria. On the eastern boundary lie Masailand and the Ngorongoro Crater.

The terrain within the park varies from the treeless, central Serengeti Plains to savannah-type stretches dotted with flat-topped acacia trees and interspersed with magnificent rock outcrops, while riverine bush, thick scrub and forest grow in the north and along the Mara River.

Although the Serengeti is best known for its magnificent lions, it contains over 35 species of plains game as well as some 350 species of birds. A wildlife population of more than 1½ million large mammals has been recorded. According to recent estimates, there are more than three million animals in the Serengeti, including 1½ million wildebeest, 750,000 gazelle and 500,000 zebra.

The annual movement in May or June of wildebeest and zebra from the central plains to the permanent water of the western corridor and their return in November or December is one of the most remarkable and inspiring sights of Africa. The great herds gather in the central plains and then move steadily westwards, six or seven abreast and often forming a line several miles long. At the tail end of the procession come the cripples and those too old to keep up, with the inevitable following of lion and other carnivores. Thousands and thousands of wildebeest and zebra pass through the central Itonjo Range, gradually dispersing throughout the length and breadth of the corridor until many are up in the northern Serengeti and move into the Mara area of Kenya.

The classic book on the Park is *Serengeti Shall Not Die*, by Dr Bernhard Grzimek, the Director of the Frankfurt Zoo. Indeed the Serengeti manages to retain the wild, untamed atmosphere of Africa as it always was, leaving even the most blasé visitor with a haunting memory of its primeval beauty.

There are several lodges in the Serengeti and many camping sites. The Seronera Wildlife Lodge (TTC), pretty well in the centre of the Park, is pleasantly built of stone, with swimming pool, shop and airstrip. The game viewing round here is renowned and at night you can hear lions roaring nearby. Land Rovers can be hired from STS and ranger guides are available. About 64 km (40 miles) from Seronera towards the Kenya border is Lobo Wildlife Lodge (also TTC), ingeniously set on a natural rock promontory, with a swimming pool, shop, airstrip and good game viewing. (Both Lobo and Seronera are due to be renovated in 1984 with the aid of the World Bank.) Fort Ikoma, a remarkable 'Beau Geste' type of fort built by the Germans in 1904, north west of Seronera, was made into a lodge but has now reverted to military use. Finally there is the Ndutu Safari Camp, 24 km (15 miles) off the Ngorongoro-Seronera road.

There are many game viewing circuits in the Serengeti, although at the time of writing driving could often be restricted by shortages of fuel. The main fuel supply is at Seronera, where cars are sometimes limited to 20 litres.

While at Seronera it is worth visiting the unique Serengeti Research Institute. This internationally staffed centre studies the wildlife and vegetation of the area, plots the migration of animals, and improves conservation methods. It is situated two miles east of the Seronera Wildlife Lodge. The Institute is closed on Sundays.

Mwanza

Immediately west of the Serengeti is the huge expanse of Lake Victoria, the second largest lake in the world and the size of Ireland. There are two towns on this side of it, Musoma and Mwanza.

Mwanza is a thriving commercial town on the shore of Lake Victoria, with low hills behind it. It is one of the principal ports of the lake and steamers call regularly. The climate is hot but not so humid as on the coast. A well-known sight near Mwanza is the Bismarck Rock, a huge rock which has been poised as if about to fall for as long as anyone can remember. There are two hotels, the new Mwanza (TTC) and the Lake (Box 910, telephone 3263), while a cheaper place to stay is the Mwanza Guest House (Box 971).

Half a mile from Mwanza, and a short boat trip away, is Saanane Island, a game sanctuary where many species of animals can be seen at close quarters. Rhino and buffalo are kept separate from the public, but antelope and other non-dangerous game are allowed to roam freely. Speke's Gulf near Mwanza is named after the explorer, who caught his first glimpse of the lake from the village of Mwanza in 1858.

A growing attraction in the area is the Sukuma Museum at Bujora about 10 km (6 miles) from Mwanza. This is the first of Tanzania's tribal museums and it has many fascinating mementoes of the chiefs and the traditional rites of the Sukuma people, Tanzania's largest tribe. Furthermore once a year, just after Saba Saba Day in July, the tribe's most famous dancers gather at Bujora for a mammoth *ngoma* or dance festival.
When in this East Lake region you can visit the famous Williamson Diamond Mines at Mwadui, though arrangements must be made well beforehand with the company. Mwadui is 137 km (86 miles) from Mwanza by road but can also be reached by air charter.

Sukuma dancers of Tanzania

Dar es Salaam

The former capital of the United Republic is a comparatively small city, attractive in appearance, with a leisurely air that belies the tremendous amount of activity going on. It has a beautiful, palm-fringed, land-locked harbour from which it takes its name, Dar es Salaam, the Arabic for 'the haven of peace', but is at the same time a busy commercial port with modern facilities, visited by the vessels of many nations. As well as serving Tanzania, the port is the shipment point for the Tazara Railway to Zambia, completed with the help of the Chinese, and also known as the Great Uhuru Railway.

Dar is a town of tree-lined avenues, Independence Avenue being a brilliant sight around Christmas time when the colourful acacias are in full bloom, full of contrasts. Modern office buildings rise next door to black-and-white painted, wood-beamed German buildings, new shops trade next door to the old shoemaker sitting on his step surrounded by pieces of leather. The city is rapidly changing and expanding, with the population expected to exceed 3,000,000 by the end of the century.

Although Dodoma will become the new capital in the late 1980s, Dar will remain the country's commercial centre and also retain the official residence of the President, State House. This lovely white Arab influenced building was the Governor's house in colonial days and stands in spacious grounds near the harbour entrance. The President has founded a private zoo in the gardens and as a result peacocks stray around the area. Note that it is forbidden to photograph any part of State House. Other historic buildings include the German administrative buildings along the waterfront, the former German club, next to the Kilimanjaro Hotel, and the small house now containing the British Council library on Independence Avenue. The old hospital an Ocean Drive is also remarkable.

The focal point of the city centre is the Askari memorial at the junction of Independence Avenue and Makataba Street, and a stone's throw from the popular open air terrace bar of the New Africa Hotel. Most of the shops are round here, so are the airline offices and banks. The main post office is a couple of hundred yards along Makataba Street. There are several chemists, including the Mahen Pharmacy, hairdressers in the Kilimanjaro Hotel and in Independence Avenue, an excellent bookshop close to the memorial, and a variety of curio shops. The great speciality of these is the carving of the Makonde tribe of southern Tanzania, who make unique pieces in ebony, both traditional and modern. The Tanzania Handicrafts Marketing Corporation's shop in the arcade of the IPS Building has a very fine display at prices far lower than in Kenya. You could pay ten times as much in Nairobi. If you become interested you should also see the Makonde ritual masks in the museum. Another speciality of curio shops is the traditional Zanzibar brass-bound chest. And of course there are game trophies. Most shops close for lunch from 12.30 to 14.00. At the time of writing there was a severe shortage of imported goods of all kinds. Camera film, for example, was unobtainable.

The National Bank of Commerce has branches in Independence Avenue and Makataba Street, while the sub office in the Kilimanjaro Hotel remains open in the afternoons.

Hotels
The Kilimanjaro Hotel (TTC, telephone 21292) stands on the Azania Front with a magnificent view over the harbour, its own swimming pool, and a nightclub. Near it is the twice enlarged New Africa Hotel (TTC, telephone 29611), originally one of three lodges built for a visit by the Kaiser before the Great War, though he never came in the end. Alas, nothing remains of the lodge, and the hotel's current expansion is incomplete. Other modern hotels include the Twiga, the Motel Agip, and the Skyways, these being less expensive, though air-conditioned. It is essential to book city centre accommodation in advance.

At the time of writing all hotels were run down and due to the shortages it was desirable to arrive with your own soap and toilet paper. However, the Kilimanjaro Hotel was due to be renovated with the aid of a World Bank loan, completion being scheduled for 1984. Almost the only hotel in Dar es Salaam which was functioning normally in 1983, and had excellent food, was the Oyster Bay Hotel, a small establishment in the picture postcard setting of a tropical, palm-fringed beach at Oyster Bay, six and a half km (four miles) from the city centre.

The beach hotels up the coast were also operating well, though they are too far out to be convenient for businessmen, but for tourists they remain viable as do the hotels in Northern Tanzania.

22 km (14 miles) north of Dar es Salaam is Kunduchi, with superb beaches and the site of the tomb of Sharifu Musa at Kondo who, it is said, was a descendant of Mohammed the Prophet. The Kunduchi Beach Hotel (TTC) can justifiably be called one of the best designed in Africa. Situated on a long, sandy beach, it was inspired by early Arab architecture and its cool white arches and terraces make a magnificent contrast to the palm trees and tropical plants around it. There is a pool-side restaurant and all rooms are air-conditioned. Close by is a local fishing village on a lagoon. Further down the beach is the brick-and-thatch Rungwe Oceanic Hotel (Box 5659 Dar es Salaam, telephone 47021).

Beyond Kunduchi is the equally fine Bahari Beach, with the Bahari Beach Hotel (TTC), based on native African designs and with one of the longest thatched roofs ever made. Its buffet food retains a good reputation.

Eating Out
Despite the country's economic problems, the rooftop restaurant at the Kilimanjaro Hotel is surprisingly good. Next after it, in our estimation, comes the Oyster Bay Hotel, which almost always has lobster on the menu. At both these places you eat in the open air: a bonus on hot evenings. Shs 200/- would buy a full dinner and Dodoma wine is usually available. For people who like a real Indian curry, there are two restaurants, the Sheeshmahal Restaurant and the Hindu Lodge at the City Hotel, though first impressions may not be inviting; for those who prefer a Chinese meal, there is a good, though seemingly unnamed, restaurant in the basement of the NIC Investment House. There are snack bars in the Kilimanjaro Hotel and at the Agip Motel.

Transport
Among car hire and taxi firms are STS, Co-Cabs, Valji and Alibhai, and Subzali Tours. You are unlikely to obtain a self-drive car.

The major tour operator is also STS, together with Bushtrekker Safaris (Box 5350, telephone 31957) and Kearline Tours (Box 1638, telephone 20607). Tour operators also have offices in the hotels, but it's worth shopping around for value among the local city tours and visits to such places as the old slave port of Bagamoyo. Another favourite tour is to the Mikumi National Park, some three hours' drive, while in the high season daily air excursions are available to Zanzibar.

Up to date information on what's on can be obtained from the Information Office of TTC on Independence Avenue.

As well as the British Council Library, already mentioned, there is an American Library on Independence Avenue and a West German Goethe Institute. The University of Dar es Salaam is very active though outside the city.

The fine National Museum in Shaaban Robert Street has relics of Chinese, Arab and Persian coastal civilisations as well as archaeological finds from Olduvai Gorge. To understand more about African life visit the traditional African village which has been built off the Bagamoyo Road, showing the various types of houses found in different parts of the country. You can often see Makonde craftsmen doing carvings, and men at work on the houses. The village is open daily, all the year, from 09.30 to 15.00.

Every year from July 1 to July 7 a National Festival Farmers' Week is held in Dar es Salaam, to coincide with the celebrations of the founding of the political movement which led Tanzania to Independence, now called the CCM, or Revolutionary Party. There are displays of tribal dancing, varying from the snake dancers of Mwanza, who use live snakes, to the weird stilt dancers of the Makonde.

Sport
There is golf, tennis and cricket at the Dar es Salaam Gymkhana Club. Fishermen should contact the Deep Sea Angling Club Secretary at the Yacht Club which is about nine km (six miles) north of Dar es Salaam.

There are safe bathing beaches near the city, the most convenient being at Oyster Bay six and a half km (four miles) and at Silversands 19 km (12 miles) to the north, and at Mjimwema south of the city for which you must cross the harbour entrance by ferry. Or there are the beaches at Bahari and Kunduchi.

Excursions
One of the best day trips from Dar es Salaam is to Bagamoyo, about 64 km (45 miles) north of Dar es Salaam, which was the terminus of the slave caravan route from Lake Tanganyika and the port of embarkation for thousands of slaves and hundreds of tons of ivory. You can still see the old stone pens where slaves were kept, and there is a shackle ring, for securing slaves, embedded in a fine old baobab tree. Several famous explorers, including

Burton, Speke and Stanley, began their expeditions into the interior from here, and there is a memorial to Burton and Speke.

In a little chapel behind the mission church of Notre Dame de Bagamoyo the body of David Livingstone once lay, after being carried across country by faithful African followers. The town, once the capital of German East Africa, is famous for carved Arab doors.

Five km (three miles) south of Bagamoyo is the picturesque village of Kaole, near which are the ruins of a mosque and pillars believed to be 800 years old.

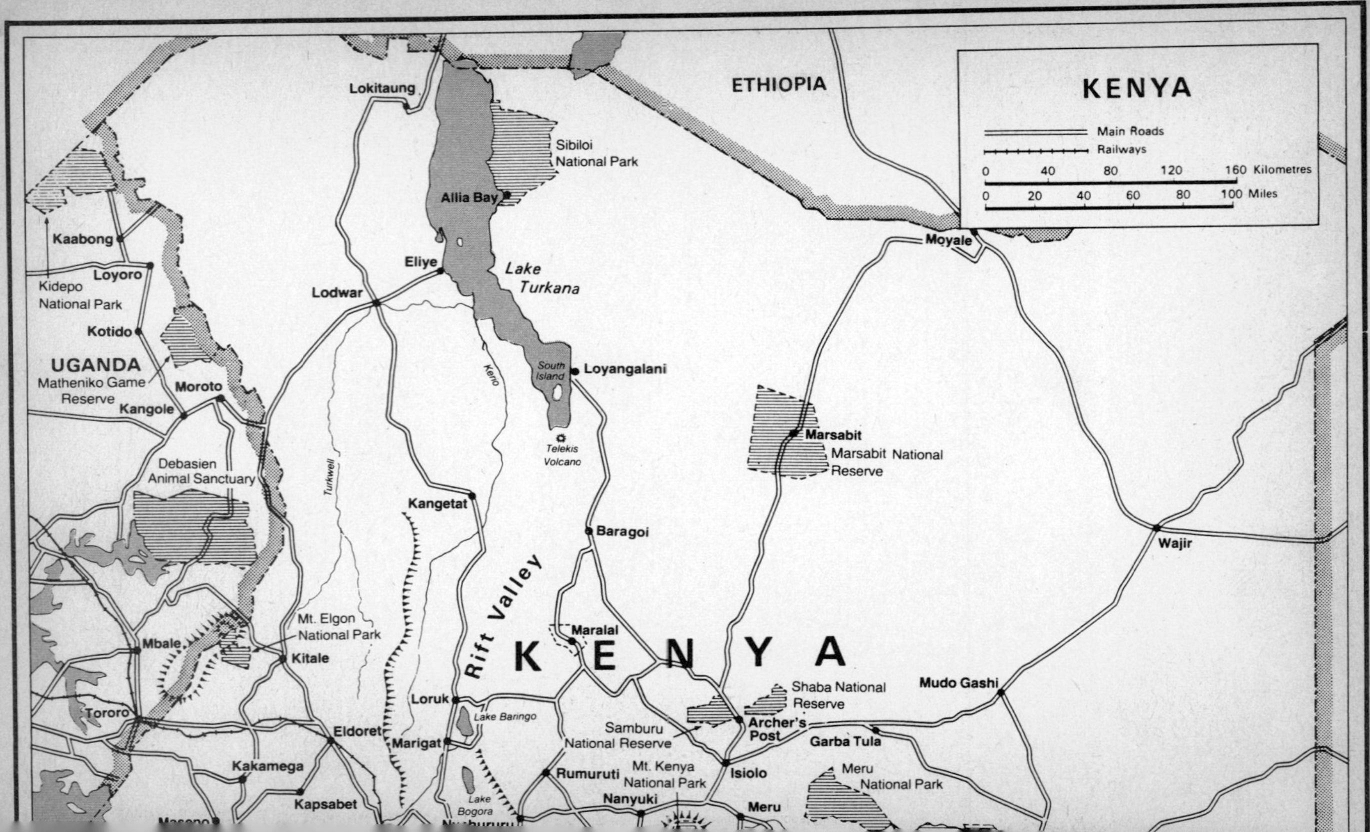
KENYA
Main Roads
Railways
0 40 80 120 160 Kilometres
0 20 40 60 80 100 Miles
ETHIOPIA
UGANDA
K E N Y A
Lokitaung
Sibiloi
National Park
Allia Bay
Lake
Turkana
Eliye
Lodwar
Kaabong
Loyoro
Kidepo
National Park
Kotido
Matheniko Game
Reserve
Moroto
Kangole
Debasien
Animal Sanctuary
Turkwell
Kerio
South
Island
Loyangalani
Telekis
Volcano
Moyale
Marsabit
Marsabit National
Reserve
Wajir
Kangetat
Baragoi
Rift Valley
Maralal
Mt. Elgon
National Park
Mbale
Kitale
Tororo
Eldoret
Loruk
Lake Baringo
Marigat
Kakamega
Kapsabet
Lake
Bogora
Samburu
National Reserve
Shaba National
Reserve
Archer's
Post
Mudo Gashi
Garba Tula
Isiolo
Rumuruti
Mt. Kenya
National Park
Nanyuki
Meru
Meru
National Park

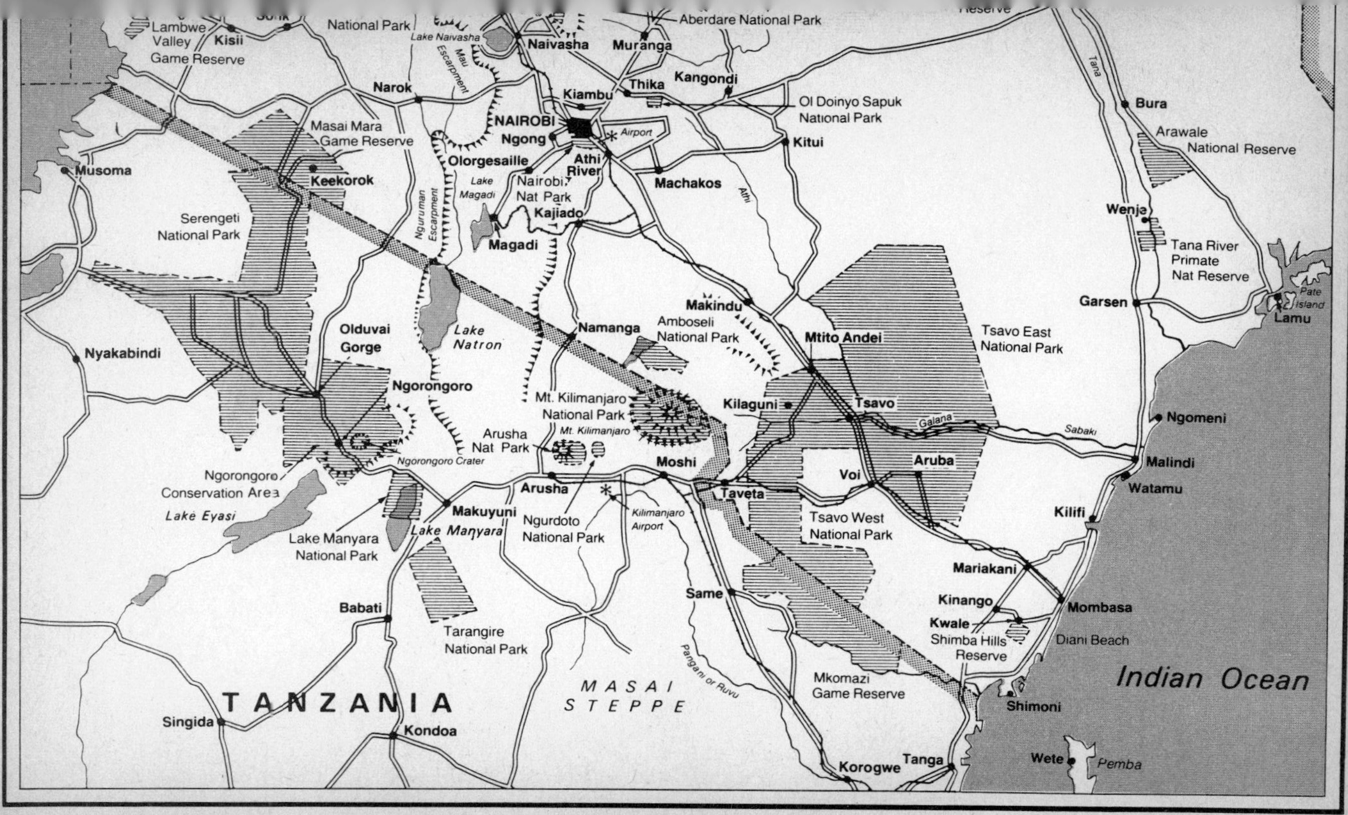
Lambwe
Valley
Game Reserve
Kisii
National Park
Lake Naivasha
Mau
Escarpment
Naivasha
Muranga
Aberdare National Park
Narok
Thika
Kangondi
Kiambu
Ol Doinyo Sapuk
National Park
Masai Mara
Game Reserve
NAIROBI
Airport
Ngong
Kitui
Olorgesaille
Athi
River
Musoma
Keekorok
Lake
Magadi
Nairobi
Nat Park
Machakos
Kajiado
Athi
Nguruman
Escarpment
Serengeti
National Park
Magadi
Tana
Bura
Arawale
National Reserve
Wenje
Tana River
Primate
Nat Reserve
Garsen
Pate
Island
Lamu
Makindu
Amboseli
National Park
Mtito Andei
Tsavo East
National Park
Olduvai
Gorge
Lake
Natron
Namanga
Nyakabindi
Ngorongoro
Mt. Kilimanjaro
National Park
Mt. Kilimanjaro
Kilaguni
Tsavo
Galana
Sabaki
Ngomeni
Arusha
Nat Park
Ngorongoro Crater
Moshi
Aruba
Malindi
Watamu
Voi
Ngorongoro
Conservation Area
Arusha
Taveta
Lake Eyasi
Makuyuni
Ngurdoto
National Park
Kilimanjaro
Airport
Tsavo West
National Park
Kilifi
Lake Manyara
National Park
Lake Manyara
Mariakani
Same
Kinango
Mombasa
Babati
Kwale
Shimba Hills
Reserve
Diani Beach
Tarangire
National Park
Pangani or Ruvu
MASAI
STEPPE
Mkomazi
Game Reserve
Indian Ocean
Shimoni
TANZANIA
Singida
Kondoa
Korogwe
Tanga
Wete
Pemba

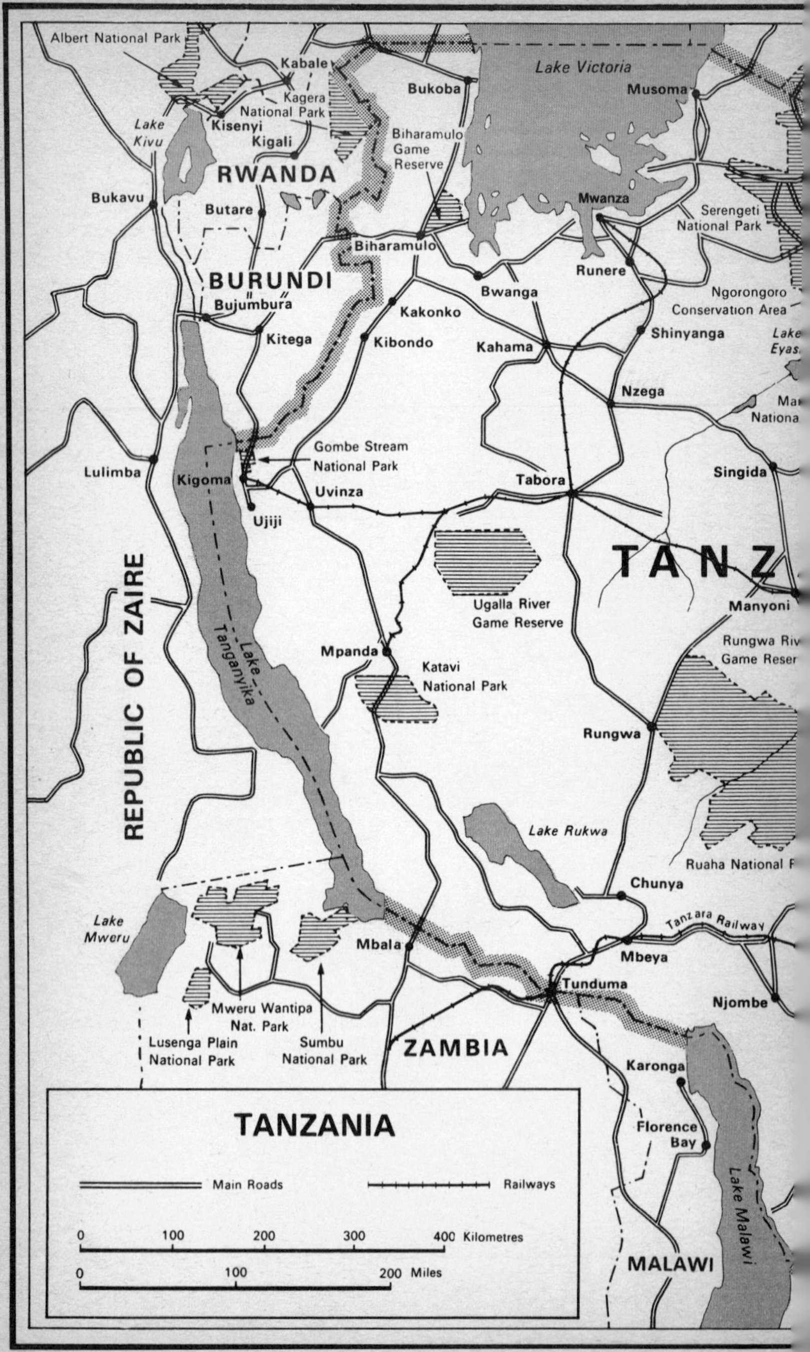

Albert National Park
Kabale
Kagera
National Park
Kisenyi
Lake Kivu
Kigali
RWANDA
Bukavu
Butare
BURUNDI
Bujumbura
Kitega
Bukoba
Lake Victoria
Musoma
Biharamulo Game Reserve
Biharamulo
Mwanza
Serengeti National Park
Runere
Bwanga
Kakonko
Kibondo
Kahama
Shinyanga
Ngorongoro Conservation Area
Nzega
Gombe Stream National Park
Lulimba
Kigoma
Ujiji
Uvinza
Tabora
Singida
TANZ
Manyoni
Ugalla River Game Reserve
REPUBLIC OF ZAIRE
Lake Tanganyika
Mpanda
Katavi National Park
Rungwa
Lake Rukwa
Ruaha National P
Chunya
Lake Mweru
Mbala
Tanzara Railway
Mbeya
Tunduma
Njombe
Mweru Wantipa Nat. Park
Lusenga Plain National Park
Sumbu National Park
ZAMBIA
Karonga
Florence Bay
Lake Malawi
MALAWI
TANZANIA
Main Roads
Railways
0 100 200 300 400 Kilometres
0 100 200 Miles

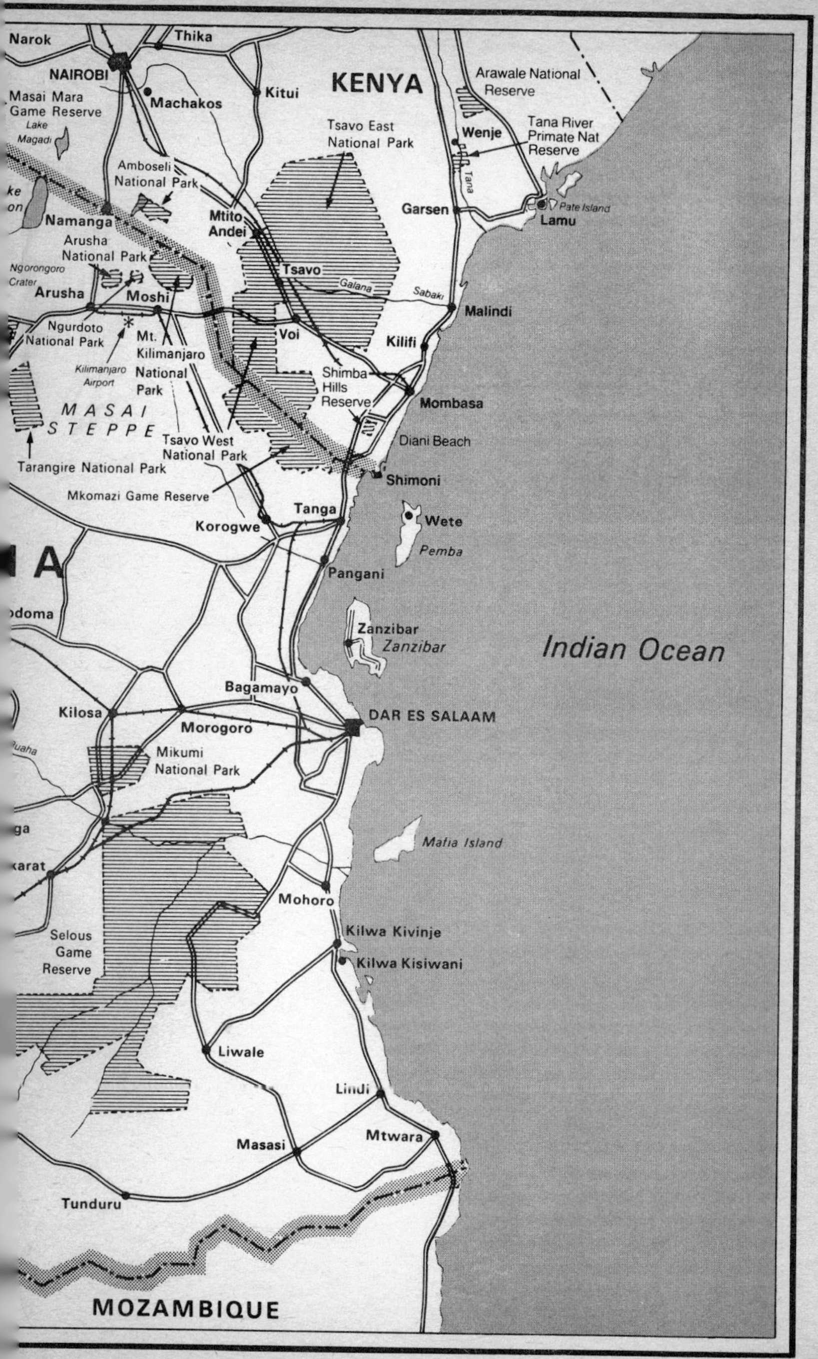

Narok
Thika
NAIROBI
KENYA
Arawale National Reserve
Masai Mara Game Reserve
Machakos
Kitui
Lake Magadi
Tsavo East National Park
Wenje
Tana River Primate Nat Reserve
Tana
Amboseli National Park
Garsen
Pate Island
Lamu
Namanga
Mtito Andei
Arusha National Park
Ngorongoro Crater
Tsavo
Galana
Sabaki
Arusha
Moshi
Malindi
Ngurdoto National Park
Mt. Kilimanjaro National Park
Voi
Kilifi
Kilimanjaro Airport
Shimba Hills Reserve
Mombasa
MASAI STEPPE
Diani Beach
Tsavo West National Park
Tarangire National Park
Shimoni
Mkomazi Game Reserve
Tanga
Korogwe
Wete
Pemba
Pangani
Zanzibar
Zanzibar
Indian Ocean
Bagamayo
Kilosa
DAR ES SALAAM
Morogoro
Mikumi National Park
Mafia Island
Mohoro
Selous Game Reserve
Kilwa Kivinje
Kilwa Kisiwani
Liwale
Lindi
Mtwara
Masasi
Tunduru
MOZAMBIQUE

Index

NOTES

NOTES